SIMPLE FRENCH COOKING
for English Homes

by X. MARCEL BOULESTIN
Introduction by JILL NORMAN

First published in 1923
This edition published in 2011 by
Quadrille Publishing Limited
Alhambra House
27–31 Charing Cross Road
London WC2H 0LS
www.quadrille.co.uk

SERIES EDITOR Jill Norman
EDITORIAL DIRECTOR Jane O'Shea
ART DIRECTOR Helen Lewis
PROJECT EDITOR Simon Davis
DESIGNER Lottie Crumbleholme
PRODUCTION DIRECTOR Vincent Smith
PRODUCTION CONTROLLER James Finan

Simple French Cooking is set in Sabon, a Garamond revival typeface by Jan Tschichold.

Cataloguing-in-Publication Data: a catalogue record for this book is available from the British Library.

ISBN 978 184400 981 7

Printed and bound in China

Contents

Introduction by Jill Norman

When Marcel Boulestin moved from Paris to London in 1906 it is reasonably certain that he had little idea of becoming a restaurateur and food writer. Born in Poitiers in 1878 he was brought up by his mother and maternal grandmother, visiting his father only in the summer at his property north of Périgueux. At school he developed an interest in theatre and music. At the age of 18, after both his mother and grandmother had died and he was left a small income, he moved to Bordeaux, intending to study law, but instead became a regular concert-goer and contributed articles to a national journal, *Courrier Musical*. After national service in 1899 he moved to Paris to become secretary to the humorous writer Willy (Henri Gauthier-Villars) and became part of the tumultuous Colette-Willy ménage. He enjoyed the anglophile society of Paris and Dieppe, became friends with several English artists and writers, translated a book by Max Beerbohm in 1905, and by now thoroughly enchanted by all things English, including some of our food, he decided to move to London.

He dabbled in journalism, translated plays and immersed himself in theatre and music, and in 1911 turned to interior design with some success. His society friends supported him, and the business was about to expand when the first World War started. Boulestin joined the French infantry and served as an interpreter for the British expeditionary force in France. When he returned to London he opened a new decorating business, but that failed badly. His ideas were too avant-garde, and by now there were many small firms of interior decorators, some set up by the society women who had been his clients. For a time he scraped by giving French lessons, editing and writing, and serving as a wine adviser to wealthy individuals. He also took to cooking for himself rather than going to restaurants, and cooked for people's dinner parties.

Simple French Cooking for English Homes was commissioned on the spot by a director of Heinemann's with whom Boulestin was negotiating the sale of some etchings by his friend J.E. Laboureur. He received an advance of £10. The book appeared in 1923 and was an immediate success. Boulestin had no formal training in cooking, but as he said 'I had eaten well all my life, and like the majority of my compatriots of the south-west, I had an instinct for cooking'. His simple dishes suited the pared-down post-war lifestyle. He emphasized that his recipes for French bourgeois family food, whose great merits were 'excellence, simplicity and cheapness' were utterly unlike the 'nondescript dishes boasting pretentious names' served in international hotels.

At about this time, Boulestin met Robin Adair, a kindred spirit with an interest in music and food; the two became life-long partners. In 1925, urged on by many of their friends, Boulestin opened a restaurant in Leicester Square, London with Adair as his partner. He engaged a well-known chef, Bigorre, from Paris and the restaurant was simply called Restaurant Français. The elegant room was devised by his artist and decorator friends to create a truly Parisian atmosphere. By now, Boulestin had published *A Second Helping*, and his articles in the *Daily Express*, *The Manchester Guardian*, *The Spectator* and *Vogue*, meant that his name was well known. There was no other genuine

French restaurant in London at that time; the better restaurants were generally huge hotel restaurants, so the Restaurant Français was a pleasant change and became an instant success with the rich and famous. It flourished for two years before moving to Southampton Street in Covent Garden where Boulestin went into partnership with Sherry's Restaurant. These bigger premises opened under the name of Restaurant Boulestin and survived, with different owners, until the early 1990s.

Through the restaurant, and through his writing—he published a dozen cookery books, some written alone, some with Adair, one with Jason Hill, between 1923 and 1937—Boulestin had a profound influence on the revival of good food after the first World War. Many of his recipes did not call for expensive ingredients and so his books sold to a wide audience. He also made a series of short films for a gas company which were shown in cinemas all over the country. From 1928 he gave cookery courses at Fortnum & Mason in Piccadilly, and in 1937 became the first TV cook.

For two years Boulestin made two 15 minute television Programmes, entitled *Cook's Night Out*, every month. These went out live from a cramped studio in which the lights and stove generated an uncomfortably high temperature, and Boulestin had to restrict his movements in order not to upset the camera focus. There was obviously a limited choice of dishes that could be prepared in 15 minutes: omelettes, crêpes, quickly prepared fish dishes like sole grillée or sole au vin blanc, some salads and sauces. Photographs of his appearances show an elegantly suited man, dressed more for going out to lunch than into the kitchen, preparing his ingredients.

Established as the expert on simple French food and cooking, his books paved the way for later 20th century writers. 'The modern cook book began in the 1920s with an immigrant Frenchman, Boulestin' wrote Matthew Fort in *The Guardian* in 1999. He was the most imaginative and liberating food writer of his time. Elizabeth David acknowledged her debt to him and wrote of 'his intelligence, sense and taste, of his ease of style, un-scolding, un-pompous, un-sarcastic, ineffusive, and to so high a degree, inspiriting and creative' (*Wine and Food*, 1965, reprinted in *An Omelette and a Glass of Wine*).

Simple French Cooking for English Families is a precise title; this is not a cookery course for beginners, but it does not demand great expertise either. Boulestin starts with some general culinary advice: 'Do not be afraid to talk about food. Food which is worth eating is worth discussing'; 'Do not be afraid of simplicity. If you have a cold chicken for supper, why cover it with a tasteless white sauce which makes it look like a pretentious dish on the buffet table at some fancy dress ball?'; 'Do not use substitutes or essences chemically made; if you want to flavour a cream with vanilla or coffee, use the vanilla pod or make yourself some very strong pure coffee'.

Boulestin also wrote 'Cookery is not chemistry. It is art, it requires instinct and taste rather than exact measurements, the only exception being for making pastry and jams, where exact measurements and weights are important'. Indeed, his recipes do not give much detail: the recipe for Maître d'Hotel Sauce says 'Put a good piece of butter in a small saucepan with a drop of water and the juice of a lemon; cook one minute and add chopped parsley and a little salt'. The essentials are there, and the cook can make the amount required, balancing the quantities of butter, water, lemon juice and parsley to achieve a good flavour and texture.

The introduction to the Salads chapter is a strong condemnation of English salads. He shuns English 'cream sauces and sham mayonnaise' and 'the addition of the fatal radish, the strong taste of which absolutely kills that of the other vegetables'. 'A salad must be fresh and crisp, its flavor sharp and appetizing', he observes and explains that French salads are of two kinds: green salads made with whatever is in season and dressed with a simple vinaigrette, and more elaborate composed salads that need a more elaborate dressing. The recipes that follow are concise in their ingredients and the type of dressing to use.

His explanations and recipes for the basic French ways to cook vegetables, fish, meat, poultry and game widened the culinary ambitions of British people who had never dreamed of being able to produce French food in their own kitchens. He encouraged his readers to adopt a lighter and more varied style of cooking, with less emphasis on large joints of meat 'with boiled potatoes and boiled cabbage', and to avoid waste—'some of our best dishes are made up of "remnants"; in fact there is no waste whatever in the French kitchen'.

His contribution to our culinary literature was to enlarge readers' confidence to extend their repertoire of recipes, calling for open-mindedness and using instinct and creativity in the kitchen. In the Introduction he urges readers to read his book in bed rather than a contemporary European travel guide. 'The one shows you all the wonderful places to which you can never afford to go; the other tells you of all the delicious dishes you can afford to enjoy and give to your friends'.

Conversion Chart

WEIGHT

½ oz	15 g
¾ oz	20 g
1 oz	25 g
1½ oz	40 g
2 oz	55 g
3 oz	85 g
3½ oz	100 g
4 oz	110 g
4½ oz	125 g
5 oz	140 g
6 oz	175 g
7 oz	200 g
8 oz	225 g
9 oz	250 g
10 oz	275 g
10½ oz	300 g
12 oz	350 g
14 oz	400 g
15 oz	425 g
1 lb	450 g
1 lb 2 oz	500 g
1¼ lb	600 g
1½ lb	700 g
1 lb 10 oz	750 g
2 lb	900 g
2¼ lb	1 kg
3¼ lb	1.5 kg
4½ lb	2 kg

VOLUME

1 teaspoon (tsp)	5 ml
1 dessertspoon (dsp)	10 ml
1 tablespoon (tbsp)	15 ml

1 fl oz	30 ml
1½ fl oz	40 ml
2 fl oz	60 ml
3 fl oz	85 ml
3½ fl oz	100 ml
4 fl oz	125 ml
5 fl oz	150 ml
6 fl oz	175 ml
7 fl oz	200 ml
8 fl oz	225 ml
10 fl oz (½ pint)	300 ml
12 fl oz	350 ml
13 fl oz	375 ml
14 fl oz	400 ml
15 fl oz (¾ pint)	425 ml
16 fl oz	450 ml
18 fl oz	500 ml
20 fl oz (1 pint)	600 ml
1¼ pints	750 ml
1⅓ pints	800 ml
1¾ pints	1 litre
2 pints	1.2 litres
2¾ pints	1.5 litres
3½ pints	2 litres
4 pints	2½ litres

LENGTH

¼ inch	5 mm
½ inch	1 cm
1 inch	2.5 cm
2 inch	5 cm
3 inch	7.5 cm
4 inch	10 cm
5 inch	13 cm
6 inch	15 cm
7 inch	18 cm
8 inch	20 cm
9 inch	23 cm
10 inch	25 cm
11 inch	28 cm
12 inch	30 cm

OVEN TEMPERATURES

The following conversions are based on a conventional oven. If you are using a fan-assisted oven, set the temperature 10° to 15°C lower.

Cool
140°C   275°F   Gas 1

Low
150°C   300°F   Gas 2

Moderately low
160°C   325°F   Gas 3

Moderate
180°C   350°F   Gas 4

Moderately hot
190°C   375°F   Gas 5

Hot
200°C   400°F   Gas 6

Hot
220°C   425°F   Gas 7

Very hot
230°C   450°F   Gas 8

Preface

FRENCH cooking is not, as some English people seem to think, complicated, rich and expensive. They must not judge it by the *table d'hôte* dinners they may have eaten, either in France or in England, where nondescript dishes boast of pretentious names, and where there is always a white sauce for the fish and a brown one for the meat. This represents only hotel cooking at its worst. Chemistry should be avoided in the home kitchen. In any case, hotel food, even when good, does not represent French cooking.

You may have tasted the cuisine I mean at some wayside inn[1] during the summer months in Touraine or Brittany, or in Périgord, where truffles grow; or even in some of the smaller Paris restaurants, if you knew how to find them. It is the cooking of the French *bourgeois* family, whose favourite proverb is *on ne mange bien que chez soi*, and its great merits are excellence, simplicity and cheapness.

I am told that English cooks always tell their mistresses that French cooking is so extravagant because "everything is cooked in pounds of butter". This, to begin with, is only partly true. Also they forget, or rather they do not know—how could they, traditionally convinced as they are that a "joint" must appear on the table at least once a day?—that every scrap is used up; that

---

[1] "What an excellent inn at Moulins."—TRISTRAM SHANDY.

some of our best dishes are made up of "remnants;" in fact, that there is no waste whatever in a French kitchen.

I am also assured that many English cooks find cooking a tedious drudgery; perhaps that is because they have no imagination, or are not given a chance of showing any initiative. It certainly must be extraordinarily dull to send up boiled potatoes and boiled cabbage meal after meal. No one could take an interest in work of that kind. They should try experiments with new dishes; they should be encouraged to do so, and neither mistresses nor cooks should despise or fear food of foreign origin, however simple or complicated. They are not afraid of it abroad ; in fact, they always remember it pleasantly. Why should not they try to have those same nice dishes in their own houses? It would make their menus more varied and their household bills infinitely lighter.

Such is the simple aim of this little guide. It has no pretensions of being a complete cookery book; indeed, more advice about steak-and-kidney pie or jam roll pudding would savour of impertinence.

Most of the recipes it contains are simple and the dishes easy to make. I had ample proof of this during the war, when I was mess president of a divisional headquarters mess. We had in succession two soldiers who had never been professional cooks (or even company cooks); one was a bricklayer, the other a greengrocer; they could do nothing except burn their ration of bacon in the lid of a biscuit tin. When on rest I told them to watch the French woman who cooked for us[1]; then they tried a few plain things, and in a week or two they were able to make some of the simpler

---

[1] "Even the headless oyster seems to profit from experience."—DARWIN.

dishes quite well. And luck would have it that the fellow used to bricks and mortar turned out to have a very light hand. Anyhow, a real cook, either amateur or professional, will have no trouble whatever in doing what they did.

I hope that these recipes will not be received by the public at large in the true Forsyte spirit,[1] but that they will be conducive to what Henry James calls "the larger latitude".

I trust that the cook, however temporary, and also the mistress, will take this book to bed at night. The latter will find it better reading even than the Continental Bradshaw: the one shows you all the wonderful places to which you can never afford to go; the other tells you of all the delicious dishes you can all afford to enjoy and give your friends.

It also contains some more elaborate recipes—recipes of quite remarkable local dishes, handed down, like Homer's verses, from generation to generation—which have not found their way yet even into French cookery books, and are entirely ignored by the chefs of international hotels. These, indeed, have been trained to cater for an "exclusive" cosmopolitan crowd with exclusively cosmopolitan tastes; the result being that you get precisely and hopelessly the same cooking in Paris, London, Monte Carlo, Biarritz or Cairo—good of its kind, good enough in any case for diners who dance between courses and want to be seen rather than eat well. So that it is hoped that this guide will be equally useful to people who have a good cook, to those who only have a plain one, and to those who have not got one at all.

[1] "No Forsyte has given a dinner without providing a saddle of mutton."—JOHN GALSWORTHY, *The Man of Property*.

Remarks

Nothing is more pleasant than to receive your friends at your table; nothing more perfect if the food is good; but nothing more painful, for them, if it is bad. How pathetic that they should at the same time long to see you and dread your cooking. Think, too, of their remarks afterwards, if they are only acquaintances.

. . .

Do not be afraid to talk about food. Food which is worth eating is worth discussing. And there is the occult power of words which somehow will develop its qualities.

. . .

Take an interest not only in the eating, but in the cooking of your food. You should know as well as your cook if and why this dish is excellent, and what is wrong with that one.

. . .

How can you expect a servant to be interested in her work and proud of the results if you yourself are indifferent to them?

. . .

Good food is more important than many so-called "important things of life." I can imagine no more charming picture than the wife seeing to the perfection of the evening meal, and the husband on his way home from the office looking forward to it. Happiness sits smiling at their table. (Fielding has described that somewhere far better than I can.)

. . .

Do not be unreasonable and suddenly announce at seven o'clock that there will be three extra people for dinner. Cooks are only human beings and cannot work miracles.

. . .

A good cook is not necessarily a good woman with an even temper. Some allowance should be made for the artistic temperament.

. . .

Punctuality should be the first rule, upstairs as well as downstairs.

. . .

Do not be afraid of simplicity. If you have a cold chicken for supper, why cover it with a tasteless white sauce which makes it look like a pretentious dish on the buffet table at some fancy dress ball?

. . .

Do not be too insular, like the Englishman who, discussing with a Frenchman the merits of various birds, said that grey-legged partridges were better than red-legged ones.

"Nonsense!" exclaimed his friend. "We, in Périgord, always use red-legged partridges for our very best *pâtés*, stuffed with *foie gras* and truffles."

"I meant better shooting," said the Englishman.

"Oh. I meant better eating," said the Frenchman.

. . .

One cannot underrate the mellowing influence of good food on civilised beings. Hence the "business luncheons".

. . .

Give your friends "something" to drink—not lemonade, which is worse than nothing, nothing meaning plain water.[1]

. . .

Do not let your servants look after the wines. Do it yourself.

. . .

The man who likes good wines is never a drunkard; his pleasure is the appreciation of quality, not the consumption of quantity, which lowers a human being to the level of a brute.

—AND SPECIAL

Do not use substitutes or essences chemically made; if you want to flavour a cream with vanilla or coffee, use the vanilla pod or make yourself some very strong pure coffee; if you want to make a jelly, use bones and calf's foot, not gelatine.

. . .

Always use the best olive oil, not the dubious product labelled "salad oil"; and red-wine vinegar instead of malt vinegar.

. . .

Do not serve red wine with fish.

. . .

Never buy ground pepper, which has little flavour, but use one of those little table pepper mills. The best is a mixture of black, white, and aromatic peppers.

[1] "Heaven sent us soda water As a torment for our crimes." G. K. CHESTERTON.

. . .

Grind your coffee fresh every time. See that the beans are dark brown. English coffee, as a rule, is never roasted enough.

. . .

Do not spoil the special taste of the gravy obtained in the roasting of beef, veal, mutton or pork, by adding to it the classical stock which gives to all meats the same deplorable taste of soup. It is obvious that you cannot, out of a joint, get the sauceboat full which usually appears on the table.

. . .

Do not forget that a sauce which has for basis butter and yolk of egg must never reach the boiling point.

. . .

When buying vegetables or fruit do not go for size. The size is obtained at the detriment of the flavour. The large carrots you find at all greengrocers are just good enough for making soup; the taste is too strong and the flesh too coarse. The small Brussels sprouts, round and with tight leaves, are far superior to the large kind, which looks (and tastes) like a diminutive cabbage. And it is almost criminal to buy a trout the size of a salmon; a trout being at its best when its weight is about a quarter of a pound.

. . .

Vegetables or fruit which are "in season" are always better than forced ones—unless you can afford first-rate *primeurs*.

. . .

Always buy fruit yourself. Do not order by telephone; you should see what you are buying. Go and pick the best. If your greengrocer does not like your ways, do not change them—change him.

Glossary

The following are expressions which will be constantly found in this book:

CONSOMMÉ: Is the ordinary clear soup made with beef and vegetables; necessary for other soups and many dishes.

ROUX: Is flour cooked in butter, to which is added consommé. There are two kinds, the brown and the white, and they are the basis of most dishes. (See SAUCES.)

JUS: A sauce obtained by melting and stewing together, very slowly, vegetables, bones, etc. (See SAUCES.)

BAIN-MARIE: Corresponds to a double boiler. The simplest way to cook *au bain-marie* is to stand the saucepan containing the ingredients to be cooked in à larger one full of boiling water.

GRATINER: To brown in the oven with breadcrumbs and butter.

CROÛTONS: Small cubes or triangles of bread fried in butter.

PURÉE: Any vegetable mashed to a smooth consistency, with the addition of butter, seasoning, and sometimes milk or *jus*.

Most of the recipes in this book are meant for four or five people, so that if you want to make the dishes for more or for less, you increase or decrease the quantities proportionately.

The invitation of a guest implies responsibility for his whole contentment while he is under our roof.
—BRILLAT-SAVARIN.

If Medicine be ranked among those Arts which dignify their Professors . . . Cookery may lay claim to an equal, if not a superior distinction; To prevent *disease is surely a more advantageous Art to Mankind than to* cure *them.*

Those in whom the Organ of Taste is obtuse, or who have been brought up in the happy habit of being content with humble fare, whose health is so firm that it needs no artificial adjustment; who with the appetite of a Cormorant, have the digestion of an Ostrich, and eagerly devour whatever is set before them without asking questions about what it is or how it has been prepared, may perhaps imagine that the Editor has sometimes been rather overmuch refining the business of the Kitchen.
— MEREDITH, *The Art and Science of Cookery,* unpublished manuscript, circa 1849-50.

Soups

WHILE the rich, grasping peasant of the North of France feeds on bread dipped in bad *café-au-lait,* and drinks weak beer,[1] the poor peasant of the Centre and the South has his rich soups and his bottle of wine.

There is great charm as well as great nutritive qualities in these soups, of which the farmers and the labourers make their evening meal—soups made of cabbage or of onions, or of mixed vegetables and salt pork, or of sorrel—though I doubt if we should like them as they do, so thick with slices of bread that the ladle stands upright in the middle of the tureen.

There it is, time-honoured *leit-motiv,* steaming on the long oak table. A bunch of garlic hangs from the ceiling, and a ham in the chimney; and the two candles in pewter candlesticks give less light than the big log fire. They sit down to it, farmer and stable boys, and women, heavily, solemnly. They do not talk much; they eat. Or, on a summer evening, they sit on low chairs outside the house, just by the door, holding a plateful on their knees. The day's work is over, the last lazy cow back in the stable after à last mouthful at the hedge. The twilight is blue and peaceful, only disturbed occasionally by the guttural song of some frogs in the ditch. The earth smells. But its perfume is not, to them, as sacred as that of the soup. . . .

[1] "Few good things come from the North."—*Old Icelandic Proverb.*

For these were and are still the traditional soups. Our versions have been adapted by the peasant women, who have adapted themselves, risen to the rank of cook, and left the fields for the country house or the provincial town. So that these admirable dishes, without having lost any of their primitive characteristic qualities, have become more civilised; they are no more a complete meal, but a pleasant and appetising prelude.

It may be of some interest to note that the *soupe aux choux* (cabbage soup) is one of the oldest in existence. It is mentioned in an ancient popular song:

> *La soupe aux choux se fait dans la marmite,*
>
> *Dans la marmite se fait la soupe aux choux. . .*

also in a book of recipes published in Paris on 12th August, 1654, entitled *Les Delices de la Campagne.* It is dedicated to the *dames ménagères* and meant for "monasteries and other religious establishments", the author being, beautifully and anonymously, a monk of the Capucin order. One cannot help doubting his fasting on Fridays.

POT-AU-FEU

Clear Soup

Put a piece of beef, a few bones and a marrow bone in salted water. Bring to the boil and skim well. Then add the vegetables: two onions, two or three carrots, one turnip, one leek, parsley, one clove and a little pepper. Let it simmer for at least six hours. Skim well again, leaving no fat

If you have by you bones, legs and neck of fowl, put them in; it will add to the flavour. Taste it and pass through a sieve. This is the real clear soup or *consommé* with which you can make many soups, and which is necessary for à large number of dishes. It is advisable always to have some ready in the kitchen. It plays a greater and more varied part than does the "stock", so monotonously used in English cooking.

. . .

All meat soups ought to be absolutely free from fat. It is not very easy to remove it while hot. The best way is to cook your soup early in the day, then let it grow cold. The fat then forms a crust which is easily removed. Then heat up the soup again.

SOUPE AUX CHOUX. I
Cabbage Soup

Take a good-sized cabbage, break off the leaves and wash them well, cut them in pieces about three inches long. Prepare the following vegetables: three or four carrots and two turnips, sliced lengthways in four pieces, one leek, one clove. Throw all this in an iron saucepan when the water is boiling. Add salt about three-quarters of an hour afterwards. Cook about two to three hours, according to what kind of cabbage you have been using.

Half an hour before serving put in the following seasoning: one slice of bacon, parsley, two heads of garlic, all chopped very fine and mixed together, salt and pepper. The soup should be boiling when you add this mixture. Stir it occasionally.

SOUPE AUX CHOUX. II

Same preparation as before, except that instead of putting the carrots, turnips and leek in the saucepan, you fry them first in fat or butter till they are brown, then throw them in, together with the fat in which they have been fried. Add the same seasoning.

SOUPE AUX CHOUX. III

Fill the saucepan with cold water and put in apiece of streaky bacon, or better still, of pickled pork,[1] about one and a half pounds in weight (wash it first in several waters to remove salt). Bring it to the boil, skim when necessary, and cook it for two hours. Then, and only then, throw in your cabbage and other vegetables (not fried in this case) and one hour and a half later your minced mixture, as explained before.

The meat is served as a separate dish. This will be shown later.

SOUPE AUX CHOUX. IV

Instead of salt pork or bacon, the bones of roasted joints can be used up for making this soup. The process of cooking is the same, but it is advisable to add two pork sausages cut in slices and slightly fried—or slices, uncooked, of the kind of larger sausage called *saucisson*, or *cervelas*, obtainable at almost any shop in Soho or Bloomsbury.

In the South of France this *soupe aux choux* is served with thin slices of stale household bread, upon which the boiling soup is poured. It is a matter of taste.

CROUTE-AU-POT

Having got your *consommé* ready, cut some pieces of bread crusts and dry them in the oven. Cut your vegetables in smallish pieces, put both vegetables and bread crusts in an earthenware pot with your *consommé*.

---

[1] See recipe for this under heading *petit salé*, page 66.

CONSOMMÉ AUX PÂTÉS

Parboil your *pâtés* (either vermicelli, spaghetti, pearls, or whatever you choose to have) in boiling salt water. Drain them well and finish cooking them in your *consommé*.

CONSOMMÉ AU TAPIOCA

Put your tapioca (not the ordinary coarse kind, but the kind that is specially prepared for the purpose) into your boiling *consommé* in the proportion of a pudding-spoonful to each person, put the lid on, cook for about eight to ten minutes and skim before serving.

SOUPE AU POISSON. I
Fish Soup

Boil one pound and a half of any white fish, cod preferably, in salted water until cooked. Then take out the fish and carefully remove skin and bones.

Boil about half a dozen medium-sized potatoes in some of the fish water till well cooked.

Boil a plateful of onions cut in slices in milk, adding a piece of bacon (to be removed before serving).

Mix together the fish, potatoes and onions, leave a certain amount of the two stocks (two-thirds of the milk to one-third of the fish-potato stock), add a piece of butter the size of a small egg, pepper and salt, and bring gently to the boil. Let it be reduced to the consistency you like. It should, however, be served rather thick.

SOUPE AU POISSON. II

Prepare as before and add, half an hour before serving, about eight oysters (being careful to put in all the sea water from the hollow shell) and a little cream.

SOUPE AU POISSON. III

Prepare as before but add, half an hour before serving, a few pieces of lobster or crab and a good pinch of saffron.

SOUPE AU POISSON. IV

Get a pound of mixed fish, one mackerel, one herring, one mullet, one whiting, a few sprats, a small piece of haddock, two or three oysters, and a small crab. Clean and wash the fish; boil the crab; put aside till wanted.

To make your stock, put into a rather flat saucepan a wineglassful of olive oil, a wineglassful of dry, white wine, a bay leaf, a little thyme, a few cloves, three heads of garlic finely chopped, and, cut in thin slices, three tomatoes, three onions, two leeks, also parsley, salt and pepper. Cook all this till brown, stirring all the time; then add hot water little by little till you get about double the quantity required. Then put in the fish and boil for about one hour with lid on.

Pass through a sieve, bring to the boil again, add a pinch of saffron, the flesh of the crab and spaghetti. Cook about a quarter of an hour, and just before serving add grated cheese.

SOUPE AU FROMAGE
Cheese Soup

When your *consommé* is ready, cut the vegetables in small pieces, put them back into the soup, add spaghetti, vermicelli, or macaroni; boil for ten minutes, then add grated cheese, Parmesan or Gruyère, and cook for another five minutes.

POTAGE CRÉCY

Begin boiling your rice in salted water and finish it in *consommé*. Make a *purée* of carrots as follows: boil the carrots together with one onion, a drop of vinegar, a pinch of sugar, salt and pepper; when cooked mash them, pass through a sieve, and add a little butter; then mix with the rice and *consommé*. This soup should be about the consistency of cream.

POTAGE A L'OSEILLE
Sorrel Soup

Take three handfuls of sorrel, clean the leaves, remove the stalks and centre ribs and wash them well. Melt them in a saucepan with a piece of butter the size of an egg; add pepper and salt and sufficient water. Dry in the oven a few very thin slices of bread. Beat the yolks of two eggs with a tablespoonful of milk and add this, stirring well, just before serving on the slices of bread.

POTAGE PARMENTIER
Potato Soup

Cook in salted water four or five potatoes of the white floury kind. Drain them and pass them through a sieve; put this *purée* in a saucepan with a little butter, a tablespoonful of milk, salt, pepper and chopped chervil. Add your *consommé* in sufficient quantity, bring to the boil and let it simmer and reduce (it should not be too thick, about halfway between a clear and a real thick soup) and serve with *croûtons*.

CRÈME AUX TOMATES
Tomato Soup

Fry in butter for a few minutes four leeks and eight tomatoes, let them simmer for five minutes; then add required quantity of water (about two pints), add about six medium-sized potatoes, salt and butter, and bring to the boil. Cook for about three-quarters of an hour; pass them through a sieve, bring to the boil again and add two tablespoonfuls of cream or milk.

POTAGE SAINT-GERMAIN
Pea Soup

Cook fresh peas in water with salt and one onion. When cooked pass through a sieve. Add some *consommé* to proper consistency (fairly thick), boil for a few minutes, then add just before serving a pinch of sugar; also a few leaves of sorrel, lettuce and chervil finely chopped, warmed in butter for a few minutes.

POTAGE AUX LENTILLES
Lentil Soup

Same preparation as before; but before serving add, instead of lettuce, sorrel and chervil, a piece of butter the size of a walnut, and the yolk of an egg beaten up with a little gravy.

POTAGE AUX POIREAUX
Leek Soup

Melt in butter (as described in *potage à l'oseille*) a handful of sorrel. Also cook slowly in a covered saucepan four leeks, four potatoes, and a good piece of butter, stirring occasionally. When cooked add water, salt, pepper, and a tablespoonful of cream. This soup can be made either rather thick, and served as it is, or rather thin—in which case you bring to the boil again ten minutes before serving and throw in a little vermicelli.

POTAGE JULIENNE

Cut in very thin slices carrots, turnips, potatoes, leeks, cabbage, onions; put them in a saucepan with three or four lumps of sugar, cover the saucepan and cook very slowly, stirring occasionally. When nearly cooked add *consommé* and finish cooking.

SOUPE A L'OIGNON
Onion Soup

Cut the onions in thin slices; melt some butter and cook them till they are a good golden brown colour. Then add a pinch of flour and sufficient water, salt and pepper, bring to the boil and cook about a quarter of an hour. Add grated cheese. Have ready some thin slices of dry bread fried in a mixture of butter and grated cheese. Pour the soup over these when ready and serve very hot.

CRÈME AUX ÉPINARDS
Spinach Soup

Prepare in exactly the same way as sorrel soup, but serve slightly thicker and without slices of bread and add a little paprika.

CONSOMMÉ FROID
Cold Consommé

Take some *consommé* and add to it a quarter of a pound of raw beef and a little chicken meat, if you have any, very finely chopped; then three tomatoes reduced to a pulp and the white of an egg. Mix well, add salt and pepper, bring to the boil, stirring well, then let it simmer for two hours. Pass through a sieve and pour it in cups. Serve cold.

TOURAIN AUX TOMATES
Clear Tomato Soup

Cut in quarters eight tomatoes, one onion in thin slices, fry these in pork fat for a few minutes; add a pint and a half of hot water, salt and pepper (a good deal of pepper); bring to the boil and keep simmering till the tomatoes are well cooked. Pass through a sieve, throw in some vermicelli and cook again for five or six minutes.

This is the traditional soup which, even now in all the Périgord, is offered to husband and wife on their wedding night. À large tureenful is brought to them in great state (and with a good deal of noise) by the neighbouring peasants, usually a few hours after the bride and bridegroom have retired. They eat it in bed; the guests watch them and finish the rest. It seems more sensible than many other old customs, such as for instance throwing rice (uncooked) at them in the street.

Sauces

I HAVE included under the above heading some sauces to be served with all sorts of fish or meat. These are not separate sauces, but part of the dishes themselves. By doing so I have been able to make the recipes more concise and to avoid repetition; the reader will only have to refer to this chapter when he comes to where I mention "cover", or " serve with"—whatever sauce it may be.

ROUX BRUN
Brown Roux

Put in a saucepan, on a quick fire, a piece of butter the size of a small egg, a tablespoonful of flour, and cook till brown; add a little *consommé,* a tablespoonful of *purée* of tomato; cook, stirring all the time till it is a little reduced, and if you like, pass through a sieve.

ROUX BLANC
White Roux

Put butter and flour as before in a saucepan on a slow fire, cook for a few minutes, add *consommé* and cook again for a few minutes, stirring all the time.

COURT-BOUILLON

Put in a saucepan two pints of water, à large onion and one carrot; cut in small pieces parsley, à laurel leaf, a little thyme, salt, pepper (coarsely broken) and a tablespoonful of red-wine vinegar. Cook for about twenty minutes. To be used for the boiling of fish.

BEURRE NOIR
Black Butter

Melt butter on a quick fire till it gets black without getting burnt. Add a few capers.

BEURRE BLANC
White Butter

Put in a saucepan two shallots finely chopped, two tablespoonfuls of vinegar, salt and freshly ground pepper. Cook a few minutes, then add about five pieces of butter the size of a walnut. Cook again, stirring with a wooden spoon for a few minutes, but do not let it boil.

BEURRE D'ANCHOIS
Anchovy Butter

Take the fillets of four anchovies, wash them, and pound them in a mortar with a good piece of butter

MAÎTRE D'HÔTEL

Put a good piece of butter in a small saucepan with a drop of water and the juice of a lemon; cook one minute and add chopped parsley and a little salt.

SAUCE BLANCHE
White Sauce

Put in a saucepan a good piece of butter, a puddingspoonful of flour, add salt and water and stir with a wooden spoon over a slow fire till nearly boiling; then add a few small pieces of butter and mix well. This sauce must be the consistency of cream.

SAUCE AUX CÂPRES
Caper Sauce

Is a *sauce blanche* with capers in it.

SAUCE ROUILLEUSE
Red Sauce

Put in a saucepan a tablespoonful of flour, an onion and two shallots finely chopped, and a wineglassful of salted water; cook for a few minutes; five minutes before serving put in the blood from the chicken or duck and cook again two or three minutes. To be served with roast chicken or duck.

SAUCE BÉARNAISE

Put into a saucepan a glass of white wine, a little tarragon, two shallots finely chopped and let it reduce to two-thirds. Have ready in a basin the yolks of four eggs, a small piece of butter and a little red pepper. Pour your sauce over this, pass through a sieve and put into another saucepan; cook gently, stirring all the time till it sets, but be careful not to bring to the boil; add just before serving chopped parsley and a few drops of lemon juice. This sauce must have the consistency of a stiff *mayonnaise*.

SAUCE AU VIN BLANC
White Wine Sauce

Make a brown *roux,* add a glassful of dry white wine and boil for a few minutes.

SAUCE PIQUANTE. I
Sharp Sauce

Chop two shallots, put them in a wineglassful of vinegar, with two tablespoonfuls of *consommé,* let it reduce, add chopped gherkins and capers, salt and pepper.

SAUCE PIQUANTE. II

Prepare as before, but add at the beginning (instead of gherkins later) a few heads of garlic cut in four pieces. Cook slowly for one hour with pepper and salt.

SAUCE TOMATE. I
Tomato Sauce

Cut four tomatoes in quarters, remove the seed, put them in a saucepan with one carrot and one onion finely chopped, salt and pepper; cover with water and bring to the boil; cook it well.

Then pass through a sieve. Add a brown *roux,* a little *consommé,* and cook again, stirring occasionally, to proper consistency. Should be fairly thick.

SAUCE TOMATE. II

Add to a little brown *roux* some tinned *purée* of tomatoes, a tablespoonful of *bouillon,* salt, pepper, very little grated nutmeg, a piece of butter the size of a walnut, and let it simmer for ten minutes.

SAUCE BORDELAISE

Chop two shallots, one small onion and three or four mushrooms, cook them for five minutes in oil on a quick fire; add a pinch of flour, a spoonful of *consommé,* a spoonful of tomato *purée,* salt, pepper and parsley, and reduce to three-quarters.

SAUCE BÉCHAMEL

Make a white *roux,* add a glass of milk, salt, pepper, and a little grated nutmeg; mix well and boil for a quarter of an hour, stirring occasionally; then add a few pieces of butter and pass through a sieve.

SAUCE SOUBISE

Cut two large onions, cook them in half water, half milk, salt, and a little nutmeg. When well cooked pass through a sieve and mix with a *béchamel* sauce. Stir well and boil for a minute or two.

JUS

Put in a saucepan carrots and onions cut in slices, enough to cover the bottom of the saucepan; then put in any odd bones and skins of any meat you may have, legs of chicken, one calf's foot, salt and pepper. Cover the saucepan and put it over a moderate fire. When all the ingredients have started melting, add a good deal of water and let it simmer for quite eight or ten hours till it is very much reduced. Skim off the fat and pass through a sieve. It must have the consistency of good milk.

SAUCE HOLLANDAISE

Boil till reduced by half two tablespoonfuls of vinegar and a little pepper. Mix in a basin the yolks of three eggs, a good piece of butter, and salt. Pour over this your vinegar and stir it over the fire till well mixed. Cook it *au bain-marie,* stirring all the time, adding small pieces of butter till quite smooth. This sauce must not be kept waiting.

SAUCE AU SAFRAN
Saffron Sauce

Make a white *roux* and prepare like a *béchamel* sauce, adding at the time of mixing a pinch of red saffron. Cook for twenty minutes. Add a few pieces of butter and pass through a sieve.

SAUCE MOUTARDE
Mustard Sauce

Put in a saucepan a piece of butter, a pinch of flour, mix well with a pudding spoon of water and the same quantity of white wine. Cook a few minutes; then put together the juice of a lemon and a liqueur glass of brandy; warm it and set it alight. Add it to your sauce and cook again for five minutes.

COLD SAUCES

SAUCE MAYONNAISE

Put the yolks of two eggs in a basin with a little salt and a drop of vinegar, and whip them well. Then put in the olive oil, drop by drop, occasionally adding a little vinegar. Always stir in the same way. Go on till you have enough sauce. This sauce should be made in a cool place.

SAUCE TARTARE

This is a *mayonnaise* to which you add mustard and chopped together parsley, gherkins, capers and tarragon. Should not be quite so stiff.

SAUCE RAVIGOTTE

Chop a hard-boiled egg and mix it well with salt, pepper, mustard, chopped parsley, oil and vinegar. The best way is to dissolve the mustard in the spoon with the vinegar. The proportions should be two spoonfuls of vinegar to three of oil—that is, if the vinegar is of average strength.

SAUCE VERTE

Chop very finely parsley, tarragon, and one gherkin; mix it with a tablespoonful of mashed potatoes, the crushed yolk of an egg; add mustard, salt, pepper, oil and vinegar. Mix vigorously.

SAUCE RÉMOULADE

Chop the yolks of two eggs, mix them with two raw ones, salt, pepper, mustard, parsley and tarragon, oil and vinegar; add chopped gherkins and capers. Mix well.

SAUCE VINAIGRETTE

Chop together very finely the yolks of two eggs, half a dozen gherkins, some capers, a few shallots, and a sheep's or calf's brain. Prepare in a basin your oil, vinegar, salt, pepper and mustard. Mix the whole thing and beat it well for some time. This sauce should be quite smooth in appearance and the consistency of thick cream. It is specially good served with hot calf's head.

Egg Dishes

THERE is really no end to the variations of this simple theme, and one could fill a volume with recipes for cooking eggs. But the simplest are really the best, and I have purposely refrained from branching off into all sorts of elaborate fancy dishes which would not be in keeping with the spirit of this book.

ŒUFS DURS
Hard-Boiled Eggs

Boil the eggs ten minutes on a quick fire; put them in cold water before using; they should not be peeled till they are completely cold.

ŒUFS DURS BÉCHAMEL

Cut them in half and cover with a *béchamel* sauce.

ŒUFS DURS A L'OSEILLE

Cut in half and serve on a *purée* of sorrel.[1]

ŒUFS DURS SAUCE TOMATE

Cut in half and cover with a tomato sauce, add triangles of fried bread round the dish.

[1] See in chapter on vegetables, *purée d'oseille.*

ŒUFS DURS AU GRATIN

Cut the eggs in two; remove the yolks and chop them with a few mushrooms, a shallot and parsley. Add a spoonful of tomato sauce, a spoonful of *consommé,* salt, pepper, a piece of butter the size of a nut and cook for a few minutes. Arrange the whites on a fireproof dish, fill them with the mixture, sprinkle with breadcrumbs, put a small piece of butter on each and brown in the oven.

ŒUFS DURS AUX ANCHOIS

Same preparation as before, but put *beurre d'anchois* instead of tomato sauce and mushrooms. Cook in exactly the same way.

ŒUFS DURS EN SALADE

Cut number of hard-boiled eggs required in quarters, chop chervil and a little spring onion. Mix well with half the number of yolks pounded and the usual seasoning of vinegar, oil, salt and pepper.

ŒUFS SUR LE PLAT

Melt a small piece of butter in a fireproof dish; break your eggs carefully, add salt and pepper. Cook over a moderate fire for a few minutes, then in the oven so that the top is properly cooked. The yolk should be quite liquid and the white set, but creamy.

ŒUFS À L'OSEILLE

Prepare a *purée* of sorrel[1] and put in a fireproof dish à layer about half an inch thick. Break your eggs over it, add salt and pepper and cook in the oven.

It is to be noted that for those egg dishes which are finished in the oven, the dish should be placed high in the oven and immediately under one of the tin plates; eggs should receive more heat from the top than from the bottom.

ŒUFS AU BEURRE NOIR

Wait till the butter is black before breaking your eggs in. Cook on a quicker fire; add two minutes before serving a few drops of vinegar, salt and pepper.

ŒUFS AU JAMBON

Cook a few thin small pieces of bacon in a fireproof dish with just a very small piece of butter. When nearly cooked break your eggs over them. Finish cooking in the oven. This dish should not be at all greasy.

ŒUFS AUX SAUCISSES

Cook a few small sausages, the kind called *chipolata,* with a little butter in a frying pan. Take a little of the fat and put it in an egg dish with the sausages and the eggs. Cook a few minutes on the fire, finish in the oven

[1] See *oseille*, page 77.

ŒUFS POCHÉS
Poached Eggs

Fill à large saucepan with salted water, add a little vinegar and bring to the boil. Break your eggs, one by one, in a bowl and drop them, also one by one, carefully into the water. Cook a few minutes only; the inside of the egg must be soft. Take them out one by one and put them for a few seconds in tepid water; then let them dry a little at the entrance of the oven.

ŒUFS POCHÉS BÉARNAISE

Poach your eggs and put them on a stiff *béarnaise* sauce.

ŒUFS POCHÉS SAUCE TOMATE

Poach your eggs and cover them with a tomato sauce.

ŒUFS POCHÉS AU JUS

Poach your eggs and cover them with *jus,* to which you add, chopped, a few leaves of tarragon.

ŒUFS POCHÉS AU MAÏS

Poach your eggs and put them on a dish of sweet corn.

ŒUFS EN COCOTTE

Put a little melted butter in a little fireproof dish and break your eggs over it, one in each *cocotte.* Cook *au bain-marie,* adding salt and pepper and, just before serving, a little tomato sauce, *jus,* or cream.

ŒUFS BROUILLÉS
Scrambled Eggs

Break your eggs in a basin, put salt, pepper, and beat them well. Put them in a saucepan with a piece of butter and cook on a slow fire, stirring occasionally. See that they do not stick to the bottom and sides of the saucepan. Add some cream before serving, mixing well.

ŒUFS BROUILLÉS AU FROMAGE

Prepare as before, adding some grated cheese at the beginning. Stir all the time. Add cream before serving.

ŒUFS BROUILLÉS AUX TRUFFES

Peel some black truffles and cut them in small pieces. Warm them in butter. Prepare and cook your scrambled eggs, add the truffles and a little *jus*. Stir well.

ŒUFS BROUILLÉS AUX CHAMPIGNONS

Peel and cut a few mushrooms. Cook them in butter, then add them to the scrambled eggs with a little cream just before serving.

ŒUFS FRITS AU SAFRAN
Fried Eggs

Fry your eggs in very hot butter, turn them, add salt and pepper, and serve them on rice covered with saffron sauce.

OMELETTE

To make a good omelette is not as easy as it seems. First of all, you must not use the frying pan for anything else; you must never wash it, only dry it with a cloth, and keep it greasy if you are not going to use it for some time (in which case it is advisable to keep it wrapped up in paper). The omelette must be cooked on a very quick fire; a few minutes are sufficient, according to the size of the omelette.

Beat the eggs in a basin (two eggs for a person) with salt and pepper. Melt a little butter in the pan, pour in your eggs and stir them with a fork. When the omelette begins to cook, shake the pan to detach it from the bottom and pass your fork round it (the omelette must not "catch" and must be free in the frying pan, so that you can move it by shaking the pan). Give it its proper form by pushing it away from you with the fork, then finish folding it and drop it on a hot dish. It is not very easy to describe the process, but it is only a knack, easy enough to acquire.

OMELETTE AUX FINES HERBES

Prepare as described above, adding in the mixture chopped parsley and *ciboules*.[1] Cook as usual.

OMELETTE À L'OIGNON

Cut an onion in thin slices, brown it in butter, adding it then to the mixture.

OMELETTE AU JAMBON

Cut some ham in very thin pieces and add to the mixture

---

[1] A very small green onion, but different from spring onion.

OMELETTE AUX CHAMPIGNONS

Cut the mushrooms in thin slices, cook them in butter, and add them to your eggs.

OMELETTE AUX POINTES D'ASPERGE

Cook the asparagus tips in butter and add as before.

OMELETTE AU FROMAGE

Add grated cheese to the eggs and beat well. Some people in this case add a little milk.

OMELETTE AUX FOIES DE VOLAILLE

Cut some chicken livers in small pieces, cook them in butter with salt and pepper. Make your plain omelette. When it is almost cooked put the chicken livers neatly in the middle, add a few drops of *jus,* and fold your omelette over them.

OMELETTE À L'OSEILLE

Prepare your eggs in a basin as usual. Get two or three handfuls of nice sorrel leaves; they should be young and fresh. Wash them well and remove the stalks and middle ribs of the larger leaves and dry them; then cut them very fine, but with a knife, not with a chopper. Mix them with your eggs, add just a little chopped garlic and chervil and make your omelette in the usual way. It should be made rather thick, so that, the inside being less cooked, the sorrel which is there remains almost raw. This gives it a peculiar acid taste, extremely pleasant and fresh.

This is the real sorrel omelette as it is done in that southern part of France where food is of the best. No omelette done with cooked sorrel can compare with it.

OMELETTE AUX POMMES DE TERRE

Cut two or three potatoes in little cubes, fry them in butter till cooked; add salt and pepper and a little parsley and spring onion chopped together. Put this in a dish, pour the beaten eggs (already seasoned) over the mixture and make your omelette.

OMELETTE AUX LAITANCES

Cook a few soft roes in butter. Prepare your eggs and make your omelette. When almost cooked arrange the roes in the middle of it and fold over.

OMELETTE AUX MOULES

Clean some mussels, put them in a saucepan in water and pepper. Boil them till they open, then remove them from the shells and cook them for a few minutes in butter with one sliced onion and a little parsley; then add to your prepared eggs.

OMELETTE AUX RILLETTES

Put in a dish a heaped up tablespoonful of *rillettes*,[1] cook them for a few minutes and drain them. Add them to your prepared mixture of eggs, salt and pepper. Mix well and make your omelette. Be careful not to put too much salt, owing to the salted character of the *rillettes*.

[1] For *rillettes,* see page 71.

OMELETTE AUX FLEURS DE SALSIFIS

This omelette is not easy to make, not because it is difficult to do it well, but because it is not easy to get the necessary flowers. Salsifis flowers are not usually sold in shops; in fact, they are only to be found in the vegetable garden in the late spring. The best salsifis for this purpose is the one imported from Spain, which has black roots and yellow flowers.

Nip them literally in the bud, and wash them well in several waters to get rid of the kind of milk which oozes out when you break them. Then dry them in a cloth for a few minutes, after which cook them in butter till they are brown, with salt and pepper. Mix them with the beaten eggs and make your omelette in the ordinary way.

Do not be surprised to see the buds open in the hot butter. It affects them more quickly than the sun; some show a few already yellow petals. It is a pretty sight; also the taste is delicious.

Fish

I. SEA FISH

MAQUEREAUX MAÎTRE D'HÔTEL
Mackerel Maître d'hôtel

Wash and clean the mackerel, dry them, then oil them and grill on a moderate fire. Put them for two minutes in a buttered dish over the fire and cover with a good *maître d'hôtel* sauce.

MAQUEREAUX FRITS
Fried Mackerel

Clean and dry the mackerel; if they are large cut them in two; sprinkle with flour and fry in butter. Both sides should be a nice golden colour. Add salt and pepper, and, just before serving, the juice of a lemon.

SARDINES GRILLÉES
Grilled Sardines

Grill the fresh sardines on a charcoal fire, well browned on each side. Serve with fresh butter.

SARDINES FRITES
Fried Sardines

Dry the sardines and sprinkle with flour; fry in very hot butter till quite brown.

The two above dishes can only be done on those parts of the coast where sardine fishing is a local industry, or in towns very near the sea. Fresh sardines get very quickly spoilt by travelling, and they have to be put in salt if they are not used at once, even for a journey of an hour or so. When really fresh they are delicious.

THON GRILLÉ
Grilled Tunny Fish

Cut a slice of tunny fish about one inch thick, season it and paint with oil. Grill it slowly, turning it over several times. Serve with a *maître d'hôtel* sauce.

CABILLAUD GRILLÉ
Grilled Cod

Cut a slice of cod, cook and serve in the same way. Add a few small steamed potatoes round the dish.

TURBOT BOUILLI
Boiled Turbot

Wash and clean the fish, seeing that no blood remains. Place it in a fish kettle in a *court-bouillon* just off the boiling point; cook it slowly without boiling, and keep the kettle closed. When cooked remove part of the *court-bouillon* so that the fish stands dry, and steam it for a few minutes. Serve with any sauce you like, *hollandaise,* caper sauce, or cold with a *mayonnaise,* to which in this case you can add two or three fillets of anchovies chopped very fine.

Cod and other white fish with a firm flesh can be treated in the same manner.

TURBOT AU GRATIN

Take pieces of cold turbot, put them in the middle of a fireproof dish, cover with a little *sauce béchamel,* breadcrumbs, and a few small pieces of butter. Surround the fish with *purée* of potatoes and bake in the oven. Serve as soon as ready.

SOLE AU FOUR
Baked Sole

Put in a saucepan a tablespoonful of brown *roux,* half a claret glass of dry white wine, three shallots finely chopped, salt and pepper, and soak this for a few minutes. At the same time have the sole cleaned and ready (the black skin should be removed) and also cook it, for a few minutes only, in an oiled fireproof dish. Then pour the sauce over it so that the fish is covered; add breadcrumbs and bake in a moderate oven for about ten minutes to a quarter of an hour, according to size.

SOLE FRITE
Fried Sole

Choose a medium-sized sole, clean it and remove the black skin, sprinkle with flour and fry in very hot oil. Dry it well. Serve with fried parsley and a lemon cut in two.

SOLE AU VIN BLANC

Put the sole in a buttered fireproof dish with a good glass of white wine and two shallots chopped. Cook five or six minutes, turning it over. Remove the sauce, put it in a saucepan and add a spoonful of brown *roux,* salt, pepper, and a few small mushrooms. Reduce it a little, pour it over the sole, sprinkle with breadcrumbs, add a few pieces of fresh butter and cook in the oven for a few minutes.

SOLE AUX FINES HERBES

Cook the sole in a dish with a little white wine and water, salt, pepper, and a sliced onion. Cook it first over the fire, then in the oven, turning the fish over so that both sides are well done. Put in a saucepan the sauce in which the fish has been cooked passed through a sieve; add a little white *roux* and a good deal of chopped parsley. Cook this for a few minutes and pour it over the sole, which, meanwhile, must be kept hot.

SOLE GRILLÉE

Prepare your sole and make a few cuts on both sides, sprinkle with salt and grill on a good fire till cooked. Prepare a mixture of chopped parsley and butter, well worked together, and pour it over the fish just before serving.

FILETS DE SOLE

These can be served in many different manners, with *sauce bérnaise, sauce crevette, sauce au vin blanc,* etc. The best way to prepare the fillets is always the same, as follows: fillet the fish and roll each fillet. Put in a dish the bones and the skin, some butter, two onions, a little white wine, salt and pepper; begin cooking over the fire, finish in the oven, basting frequently. You can, if you like, stuff the fillets with a mixture of a little white fish and mushrooms chopped together. You can also serve these fillets simply with the sauce in which they have been cooked passed through a sieve.

ROUGETS GRILLÉS
Grilled Red Mullet or Gurnet

Clean the fish, dry them, make a few cuts, season with pepper and salt, paint with oil and grill on a moderate fire. Serve with a *maître d'hôtel* or a *beurre blanc* sauce.

Grey or red mullet, brill, gurnet, herring, can be Grilled in the same way. Herring is best with a mustard sauce.

ROUGETS AU BEURRE

Clean the mullet and put them in a well-buttered fireproof dish; add salt and pepper and a few small pieces of butter between them. Cook twenty minutes in a moderate oven.

CREVETTES
Prawns

Prawns should be thrown into boiling water, with salt and parsley, and cooked four or five minutes, skimming meanwhile.

HOMARDS ET LANGOUSTES
Lobster and Crayfish

Cook in the same way, twenty minutes for a lobster, about half an hour for a crayfish.

Both are served cold with a sauce, *mayonnaise, tartare,* or with oil and vinegar and a vegetable salad.

HOMARD AU GRATIN

Cook several small lobsters; when cold cut them in two, remove the flesh, also the flesh from the claws. Chop it with the *coral*, a few mushrooms, add salt and pepper, a little butter, a tablespoonful of *jus* and cook for a few minutes. When reduced to the proper consistency fill the shells with the mixture, sprinkle with breadcrumbs, add a few small pieces of butter on the top and brown in a moderate oven.

HOMARD À L'AMÉRICAINE

Take two or three small lobsters, cut them in five or six pieces and break the claws in two.

Put into a saucepan two or three onions and the same number of carrots, with a piece of butter, the size of a walnut, and a spoonful of olive oil; cook this for five minutes. Put in the pieces of lobster, cook another five minutes; add a glass of brandy, light it and let it burn a little; then add a glass of white wine, curry powder, red pepper, salt, chopped parsley, and a heaped up spoonful of thick *purée* of tomatoes. Cover the saucepan and cook one hour on a moderate fire. Five minutes before serving add a little brandy and white wine. This dish must be very spicy.

COQUILLES ST. JACQUES
Scallops

Wash the scallops well, boil them in salted water, take them out and chop the red part and the white together with two mussels, one onion, and parsley; add breadcrumbs, a small piece of butter, half a spoonful of the water in which the scallops have boiled, salt and pepper, and cook a quarter of an hour. Fill the shells with this mixture, sprinkle with breadcrumbs, add a small piece of butter on the top and brown in a very hot oven.

MOULES À LA BORDELAISE
Mussels Bordelaise

Clean the mussels, open them by boiling them in salt water. Remove them, break off the one of the two shells which is empty, and pass the water through a fine sieve. Make an ordinary brown *roux*. Add a good spoonful of thick tomato *purée*, and, chopped together, one head of garlic, a slice of stale bread, and parsley. Season well, put the mussels in a saucepan with this mixture, stirring well, and cover with some of the water in which they have boiled. Cook a quarter of an hour.

MOULES SAUTÉES

Clean and open the mussels as described; remove them, throw away the empty shells and fry in a pan with butter, salt and pepper, one shallot, and one head of garlic, and parsley finely chopped, and a few breadcrumbs. Shake the pan well while they are cooking.

MOULES MARINIÈRE

Clean the mussels. Put them in a saucepan with one onion, one head of garlic, and parsley chopped finely together, salt and pepper, a small piece of butter, and a glass of white wine. Cook about a quarter of an hour on a quick fire.

II. FRESH-WATER FISH

TRUITES AU VIN BLANC
Trout

Cook the trout in a *court-bouillon,* to which you add a good glass of white wine. Time of cooking according to size. Drain the fish well. Serve covered with a *beurre blanc* sauce.

TRUITES MEUNIÈRE

Clean the trout, dry them and sprinkle with flour. Fry in butter till well brown; add salt and pepper. Serve with some of the butter and the juice of a lemon.

TRUITE SAUMONÉE MAÎTRE D'HÔTEL

Quite a good dish can be made of tinned salmon-trout. Before opening the tin put it for twenty minutes in hot water. Then pour the contents into a fireproof dish with butter and cook for a few minutes. Cover before serving with a *maître d'hôtel* sauce.

PÂTÉ DE SAUMON

Take two pounds of salmon, cut the best part of it in slices about one inch thick, and put them in a flat dish for two hours with a glass of sherry, salt and pepper. Mince very finely together the flesh of any white fish, a small slice of stale bread, a little of the salmon, add salt and pepper and a piece of butter the size of half an egg, and pass through a fine sieve. Peel a few truffles and chop the peelings. Add them to the mince with the yolks of two eggs and the sherry in which the salmon has been soaking. Place in a buttered pie dish fillets of salmon and stuffing alternately, and here and there a slice of truffle. Cover with ordinary pie batter and cook one hour and a quarter in a moderate oven. Serve cold.

CARPE À LA BOURBONNAISE

Cut in thick slices a carp about two pounds in weight (the roes to be kept for another dish). Add the same weight of onions cut in round slices. Brown the whole in butter and add a glass of water and half a botttle of claret; salt and pepper. Let it simmer for about four hours. Serve in a hollow dish with pieces of bread fried in butter round it.

CARPE FARCIE
Stuffed Carp

Clean the fish well. Chop together a slice of stale bread, one hard-boiled egg, two small onions, a few leaves of sorrel, a good piece of butter, salt and pepper. Mix this stuffing well and put it in the fish. Wrap it in oiled paper and cook in a moderate oven. The time of cooking depends on the size of the carp. It can also be cooked in butter and white wine, basting occasionally.

ŒUFS DE CARPE
Carps' Roes

Leave the roes one hour in cold water. Dry them. Cook them in butter with a little Madeira wine, one onion finely chopped, and very little nutmeg till nicely brown. Serve on slices of bread fried in butter.

MATELOTE D'ANGUILLES
Stewed Eels in Claret

Cook in butter half a dozen small onions cut in two; add a tablespoonful of flour. Boil, in another saucepan, two parts of water to one part of red wine. Pour the boiling mixture on the onions, add salt and pepper, half a dozen prunes, cut in two and stoned. Let this simmer about one hour and a half. Add your fish, cut in slices, about twenty minutes before serving. Surround the dish with *croûtons*.

LAMPROIE À LA GIRONDINE
Stewed Lamprey

Hang the lamprey for a couple of hours and throw it in boiling water. Wash it well, clean it and cut it in slices about two inches thick. (Throw away the head.) Wash and prepare about five leeks, keeping only the whitest part, one leek to each piece of lamprey. Cook both fish and vegetables in oil till it begins to get brown.

Boil two-thirds of a bottle of red wine and a glass of brandy, set it alight if possible for a little while; add a glass of hot water, salt, pepper, parsley, thyme, bay leaf; put in the pieces of lamprey and leeks and simmer for six hours. Before serving remove such things as the bay leaf, parsley, and thyme. Add fried bread round the dish if you like.

Meat Dishes

THIS chapter is only meant to be an addition to the corresponding chapter in cookery books, and I shall only mention dishes cooked in a manner which differs, however slightly, from the English way. The truly British roast beef is in France *Côte de Bœuf à l'anglaise,* and very much the same; but a head of garlic inserted near by the bone in a roast leg of mutton just makes all the difference in the world. I shall also deal with dishes typically French, which are usually "not quite right" in England, probably because they have been "adapted"—and therefore spoilt—by Swiss cooks; also with several dishes which are not well known, even in Paris.

HOW TO USE UP BOILED BEEF

BŒUF BOUILLI EN SALADE

If you have been making soup you will find left in the saucepan some quite good pieces of meat, and, among vegetables, carrots and turnips. Cut the vegetables and the meat in small cubes, also the white of one hard-boiled egg and spring onion or shallot finely chopped; and make a sauce as for a salad (oil, vinegar, pepper and salt), but thickened with the crushed yolk of the egg and mustard. Stir well and use as *hors d'œuvre.* You will find this dish very useful if your meal is a little "short".

BŒUF BOUILLI SAUTÉ

Cut the beef in small cubes, also cut a dozen small onions in slices. Brown the onions first in butter or dripping, then add the meat also, salt and pepper and chopped parsley. Fry till nicely brown, stirring well. You can, if you like, add potatoes cut in cubes, in which case it is better to begin cooking the potatoes for a few minutes before adding the rest.

BŒUF BOUILLI GRILLÉ

Cut your beef in slices about three-quarters of an inch thick and grill them on a moderate fire. Serve with a mustard sauce, or tomato sauce, or *maître d'hôtel,* spread over the slices.

BŒUF BOUILLI AU GRATIN

Mince a few onions and cook them in butter; cut your beef in thin slices, cook them for a few minutes, add a tablespoonful of *consommé,* a little tomato sauce, salt, pepper, parsley and garlic finely chopped. Put in a fireproof dish, sprinkle with bread-crumbs, add a few small pieces of butter and cook in the oven till well brown.

BŒUF BOUILLI BORDELAISE

Cut some onions in thin slices, brown them in butter, add to this the beef also cut thinly, add salt, pepper, a tablespoonful of *consommé,* a wineglass of white wine, a little garlic and parsley chopped, a little more butter, and cook for a few minutes more. The sauce should be reduced by a quarter.

CROQUETTES

Not only boiled beef, but any roast meat left over can be used for this. Mince well and add about the same amount of cold mashed potatoes. Brown a few sliced onions, which you add to it. Roll in flour and fry as fritters. Serve with a *sauce piquante*.

HACHIS PARMENTIER

Melt a good piece of butter, add parsley, three small onions, or à large one, and shallots all chopped together. When cooked, put in your cold meat (anything leftover from different dishes will do), salt and pepper, stir well and cook for a little while. Butter a fireproof dish, put in your mixture, cover with potato *purée* and brown in the oven.

BŒUF À LA MODE

Take a good piece of beef, beat it, flatten it, roll it and tie it. Put in here and there small pieces of bacon, about an inch long and a quarter of an inch thick (this is easily done with a special skewer called *lardoir,* which plays the part of a needle), sprinkled with salt and pepper.

Put into a saucepan onions and carrots cut in round pieces, skins of bacon and a calf's foot; stand the beef on this layer, cover the saucepan and cook for about twenty minutes on a moderate fire. Remove from the fire, add a liqueur glass of brandy, a glass of claret, a little parsley and enough *consommé to* cover the meat. Cover again and simmer for three or four hours. Remove the string. Place the carrots and onions round the meat, and pour the sauce over.

FILET DE BŒUF RÔTI
Roast Fillet of Beef

Take a nice fillet of beef or undercut, remove the skin and fat, tie it in a nice shape and insert here and there little bits of bacon fat (as explained in previous dish), add salt and pepper and bake it, basting it often. Remove the string before serving and the fat from the gravy.

This can be served with a watercress salad and potatoes, or with a white wine sauce, to which you add a few chopped truffles.

ENTRECÔTE BORDELAISE

Your beef should be about one inch and a half thick. Sprinkle with salt and oil it; grill it on a moderate fire.

Put in a small saucepan a chopped shallot and half a glass of white wine. Cook it so that it is reduced to a spoonful. Also poach the marrow of a bone, and cut it in slices. Add them to the sauce with a little piece of butter, seasoning, and a little chopped parsley. Cook for a few minutes and put it over the *entrecôte*.

ENTRECÔTE MAÎTRE D'HÔTEL

Grill as before, and pour over the *entrecôte* a *maître d'hôtel* sauce.

ENTRECÔTE BÉARNAISE

Same as before, but with a *béarnaise* sauce.

ENTRECÔTE AU BEURRE D'ANCHOIS

Same, but serve with a *beurre d'anchois.*

TOURNEDOS AU FOIE GRAS

Cut some undercut of beef in small pieces, about one inch thick, brown them ina frying pan, using a mixture of oil and butter, salt and pepper. In another saucepan warm some slices of *foie gras* of the same size and shape. Dry the *tournedos,* cover them with the *foie gras* and a good white wine sauce well reduced. Serve with fried bread.

BLANQUETTE DE VEAU

Cut some veal in equal pieces, put them in a saucepan with water, salt, pepper, carrots, onions and parsley. Bring to the boil and skim well several times. When cooked put aside.

Put in a saucepan a spoonful of flour, a piece of butter the size of half an egg; stir well over the fire, add about a pint of the water in which the veal has boiled and cook till reduced by a quarter. Then add the pieces of veal (not the vegetables).

Prepare in a basin a mixture of two yolks of eggs, a small piece of butter and half a spoonful of vinegar; mix well and add the other gravy little by little. Put it all back in the saucepan and cook for a few minutes, shaking it occasionally. Be careful that it does not reach the boiling point. You can, if you like, add a few small mushrooms.

VEAU AUX TOMATES

Cut the veal in pieces and brown it well in mixture of butter and oil. Add a chopped onion, a little flour, a tablespoonful of gravy, a tablespoonful of thick tomato *purée,* salt and pepper, cover the saucepan and simmer for at least one hour and a half.

CÔTELETTE DE VEAU MAÎTRE D'HÔTEL

Get some veal chops, remove part of the fat, paint over both sides with melted butter, add salt and grill on a moderate fire. Serve with a *maître d'hôtel* sauce.

CÔTELETTE DE VEAU AU BEURRE

Fry your chops in butter. When cooked remove them and keep them hot. Mix in a basin the yolk of one egg, a drop of water and a teaspoonful of vinegar, salt and pepper. Beat this well and pour it little by little in the butter. Cook by the side of the fire till hot. Be careful not to let it boil. Pour this sauce over the veal chops.

CÔTELETTE DE VEAU PROVENÇALE

Cook your chops as in last recipe and finish cooking in a *vin blanc* sauce, to which you have added a few shallots and garlic finely chopped and a little tomato *purée*.

CÔTELETTE DE VEAU À LA CRÈME

Cook your chops in butter. Remove them and add to the butter a spoonful of cream and the juice of a lemon. Brown well and pour over the chops.

CÔTELETTE DE VEAU PÉRIGOURDINE

Prepare your chops and beat them well, add salt and pepper and grill them on a moderate fire (preferably of charcoal). Chop together finely a rasher of rather fat bacon, one head of garlic, chervil, about ten shallots, salt and pepper. This should be ready, so that when you turn the chops to cook the other side you can cover the first side thickly with this mixture. The heat melts the bacon fat, and by the time the other side of the chop is Grilled the mince is as it should be. The dish should be served at once.

BROCHETTES DE VEAU

Cut some lean veal in pieces, about one inch and a half square, also squares of thin streaky bacon of the same size, put through a silver skewer alternately (if you have no silver skewers, use a thin wooden one), salt and pepper and grill for a few minutes.

BROCHETTES DE FOIE DE VEAU
Veal Liver

Prepare and cook as before, using calf's liver instead of veal. You can also make a mixture of both. This should be served with fried potatoes.

VEAU RÔTI
Roast Veal

Get a good piece of veal, bone it, tie it; add salt and pepper and cook well in the oven. The flesh should be absolutely white. Before cooking put in a spoonful of water and a teaspoonful of vinegar. Baste occasionally. Remove the string before serving and the fat from the gravy.

ESCALOPES DE VEAU SAUTÉES

Cut slices of lean veal, about one inch thick, beat them well and season with salt and pepper. Brown in butter on a quick fire, cover the saucepan and let it simmer a little. Add a glass of *jus* and cook till there is only enough gravy left to cover the escalopes.

They can be served like this, or with a *sauce soubise* or a mushroom sauce.

ESCALOPES DE VEAU À LA CRÈME

Prepare as before, then remove them and pour over them a liqueur glassful of brandy, set them alight, then put them back in the saucepan, add a tablespoonful of brown *roux* and a tablespoonful of cream. Cover the saucepan, cook for about one hour in a moderate oven, basting occasionally.

TÊTE DE VEAU VINAIGRETTE
Calf's Head

Put the calf's head in cold water for three hours; then tie it in a cloth and cook in a *court-bouillon*. The *bouillon* should cover the head, even at the end of the cooking: that is, four hours later. (The brains should be cooked separately, in another *court-bouillon,* for only about half an hour, according to size.) Drain well, remove the bones, cut in large pieces and serve with a *vinaigrette* sauce (the brains being used for the making of the sauce, as explained before).

FOIE DE VEAU SAUTÉ
Fried Liver

Cut the liver in slices, about half an inch thick, fry in butter and oil mixed, adding a pinch of flour, a small glass of white wine, a shallot, a head of garlic, chopped with parsley, salt and pepper. Cook on a slow fire for half an hour.

RIS DE VEAU À L'OSEILLE
Sweetbread

Keep the sweetbread in cold water for one hour, clean it, poach it in hot salted water for five minutes and let it get cold.

Put in a saucepan à layer of carrots, onions, bits of bacon and bones; put the sweetbread on it, add salt and pepper, cook twenty minutes on a moderate fire, cover with oiled paper and finish cooking in the oven. Baste often. The sweetbread should be nicely brown. Serve on a *purée* of sorrel. [1]

LANGUE DE VEAU SAUCE PIQUANTE
Braised Tongue

Put the tongue in hot water, dry it and remove the skin. Prepare in a saucepan à layer of vegetable and bacon, as in previous recipe. Add a glassful of *consommé,* parsley, salt and pepper; put in the tongue, cover the saucepan and cook on a slow fire for about three hours. When cooked, cut the tongue in slices and cover with a *sauce piquante.*

[1] See *purée d'oseille,* page 79.

LANGUE DE VEAU SAUCE TOMATE

Same preparation as before, but serve with a tomato sauce.

VEAU BRAISE AUX CAROTTES
Braised Veal

Take a good piece of veal, about three pounds in weight, brown it both sides in butter. Put in a fireproof dish eight carrots cut in round pieces, about half an inch thick, half a dozen small onions, parsley, salt and pepper, and a piece of rind of bacon; add a tablespoonful of water and white wine in equal parts, cover the dish and cook on a slow fire for about three and a half hours. Shake the dish occasionally, but do not remove the lid.

RÔTI D'AGNEAU À LA MIE DE PAIN
Roast Lamb

Roast the lamb in the ordinary way. Chop together two slices of stale bread, parsley, two heads of garlic (or better still, young garlic shoots), add salt and pepper. Spread this mixture on the lamb, baste with the gravy and cook another quarter of an hour, so that the mince is a nice golden colour.

GIGOT DE MOUTON RÔTI
Roast Mutton

Trim a leg of mutton, sprinkle with salt and insert two heads of garlic near the bone. Baste often while in the oven. Should be slightly underdone. Remove the fat from the gravy before serving.

GIGOT À LA BOURBONNAISE
Baked Mutton

Cut some potatoes in round slices, about a quarter of an inch thick, and put them with salt and pepper, one small chopped onion and the trimmings from the leg of mutton, in a fireproof dish. Make à layer about one inch thick, putting here and there little pieces of butter. Put the mutton over this and cook in the oven. Serve in the same dish.

ÉMINCÉS DE MOUTON SAUCE PIQUANTE

Cut slices of cold roast mutton, warm them in butter and serve covered with a *sauce piquante*.

HACHIS DE MOUTON

Chop à large onion and brown it it butter. Also chop the remnants of cold roast mutton, using only the lean parts, add salt, pepper, a tumblerful of *consommé*, some of the gravy, if any left, and cook slowly for about half an hour. Can be served with fried bread round the dish or poached eggs on the top.

ROGNONS EN BROCHETTES
Grilled Kidneys

Clean the kidneys, remove the skin, the fat and the nerve in the middle; slice them in two sideways, but without parting the two pieces. Put through a silver skewer. Salt and paint with melted butter. Grill for a few minutes. When ready, serve with a *maître d'hôtel* sauce, or put on each the following mixture: a piece of butter the size of a walnut, a little parsley and quarter of a head of garlic, well worked together.

ROGNONS SAUTÉS AU VIN BLANC
Kidneys au vin blanc

Clean the kidneys and prepare them; cut in thin slices. Brown them in butter on a quick fire; add a pinch of flour, salt and pepper, a little *consommé,* a half glass of white wine or pale sherry. Cook only a few minutes and serve.

CÔTELETTES DE MOUTON SAUTÉES

Clean the cutlets, remove the fat and skin and brown them in butter. Put in a saucepan a tablespoonful of *consommé,* same amount of tomato *purée,* a little red pepper and salt. Cook this about twenty minutes. Serve this on the cutlets.

CERVELLES AU BEURRE NOIR
Sheep's Brains

Put the brains for about one hour in cold water, cook them for about twenty minutes in water, salt and broken pepper, one onion, parsley, and a few drops of vinegar. Drain them well, cut in two, serve them with a *beurre noir* sauce, to which you add a little lemon juice or a few drops of vinegar.

CERVELLES MAÎTRE D'HÔTEL

Prepare as before, and serve covered with a *maître d'hôtel* sauce.

CERVELLES FRITES
Fried Brains

Prepare as before, dip in batter. Fry in very hot fat. Serve with a tomato sauce in a sauce boat.

RÔTI DE PORC PÉRIGOURDINE
Cold Roast Pork

Take a piece of pork about four or five pounds in weight (without that skin which, in the English way, becomes the crackling), remove the bones, flatten it, sprinkle freely with salt and pepper, add two or three pieces of garlic, roll it, give it a nice shape and tie well with string all round. Put it in a fireproof dish with a tumblerful of water. Sprinkle again with salt and pepper. (This dish should be highly seasoned.) Cook in a moderate oven, basting occasionally. Remove the string and serve cold in the same dish. The water and the juice from the meat should have formed a thick gravy covered by a thin layer of fat. Spread a little of this mixture on each slice of pork.

There is only one kind of vegetable to serve with this dish: that is, fried potatoes, and, if you like, a plain green salad.

CÔTELETTES DE PORC GRILLÉES
Grilled Pork Chops

The pork chops should be rather thin; clean them, flatten them and add salt and pepper. Grill on a moderate fire, turning them several times, as pork should be well cooked. Serve with a *maître d'hôtel* sauce.

PETIT SALÉ AUX CHOUX

Take a piece of *petit salé*.[1] Wash off the salt; put it in a deep saucepan with water and cook for about two hours; then add a good-sized cabbage cut in pieces, one carrot, half a dozen round potatoes, and finish cooking till the vegetables are ready. Squeeze the cabbage leaves in a sieve, put them in a dish, the pork over it, and the potatoes round. The *bouillon* can be used for making soup.

SAUCISSES
Sausages

As the sausages one buys now are usually made up of all sorts of things which ought never to be there, it is advisable to make your own sausages. This is a very simple matter.

Mince and mix well together three-quarters of a pound of lean pork, a quarter of a pound of ham, a quarter of a pound of pork or bacon fat, season well with salt and pepper, and force the mixture into a sausage skin. They will be better kept a day or two.

SAUCISSES GRILLÉES

Prick them in a few places with a pointed knife and grill well for a few minutes. Are specially good served on a *purée* of green peas.

[1] See *petit salé,* how to prepare it, page 66.

SAUCISSES AU VIN BLANC

Cook the sausages in the oven. Brown in butter an onion finely chopped, add a pinch of flour, a spoonful of *consommé,* a spoonful of white wine, salt and pepper, cook for a quarter of an hour, add just before serving a little more butter and lemon juice. Cover the sausages with this and serve very hot.

POULE FARCIE. I
Stuffed Chicken

Choose a rather fat fowl. Truss it and keep the liver. Prepare the following mixture: minced together, a good slice of stale bread, a rasher of bacon, the bird's liver, parsley, two shallots, two heads of garlic; add salt and a good deal of pepper. Beat an egg and add it with a tablespoonful of *consommé* to the mince. Work it well together and stuff the fowl. Sew the cut you have made.

Boil it in a *soupe au choux*[1] which has about one hour more to cook. It must be just on the boil.

POULET FARCI EN DAUBE. II.

Prepare a tender chicken exactly as indicated above; but instead of boiling it, cook it in the following manner: brown it well in butter and put it in a fireproof dish on a bed of small onions, slices of carrots, parsley, bits of bacon rind. Add salt and pepper and cook for half an hour on a moderate fire. Then add a glassful of *consommé,* cover the dish and let it simmer for about three hours. When cooked, remove the chicken and squeeze all the vegetables in a sieve to obtain the gravy.

[1] See page 10.

POULET RÔTI

Birds should be roasted in front of a clear fire.

POULET SAUTÉ

Take a medium-sized chicken, and cut it, making two pieces of each leg and two of each wing, and divide the rest in about six pieces.

Cut about a pound of potatoes in small pieces, and two large onions (or six small ones) in thin slices. Melt a good piece of butter or some dripping in a frying pan, and when hot put in the chicken and vegetables, salt and pepper. Stir well and often. Fry till nicely brown. Drain well before serving.

POULET SAUTÉ AU VIN BLANC

Prepare as before, but without potatoes, and fry in butter. Prepare in small saucepan a spoonful of *consommé*, a glass of white wine, a pinch of flour, and cook for a few minutes. Add this to the chicken about a quarter of an hour before serving. Pour the gravy over the pieces of chicken.

POULET SAUTÉ BORDELAISE

Put the pieces of chicken in a dish and brown it in oil, add salt, pepper, a shallot and a head of garlic finely chopped; a tablespoonful of *consommé*, one of tomato *purée*, and a few small mushrooms. Cover the dish and cook slowly for about one hour.

POULET EN CASSEROLE AUX CÈPES

Take a medium-sized chicken and stuff it with sausage meat, and put it in a fireproof dish on a bed of carrots, onions, bones and bacon rind, well seasoned. Cook for half an hour on a small fire. Add a tablespoonful of *consommé* and go on cooking for two hours.

Brown in butter, or oil, half a pound of the kind of mushrooms called *cèpes*.[1] Remove the chicken from the dish, crush the vegetable through a sieve, put back the chicken in the dish; add the gravy and the mushrooms and let it simmer for another half hour.

POULET AU GRATIN

Cut in small pieces the meat left of a roast chicken, put them in a fireproof dish and cover with a *béchamel* sauce and grated cheese, surrounded by *purée* of potatoes. Brown in the oven.

BROCHETTES DE FOIES DE VOLAILLE
Grilled Chicken Livers

Cut the chicken livers in squares, the same number of thin slices of bacon, one between each piece of liver on a silver skewer. Cook on a slow fire, turning many times. Serve with *maître d'hôtel* sauce.

---

[1] The large fungus which grows in oak forests. They are not *all* poisonous. It might not be advisable to pick them yourself in the season, but the preserved ones are quite safe. They are sold at most of the big stores and all the Soho shops.

DINDE TRUFFÉE
Stuffed Turkey

Take a well-fattened turkey. Get a pound of truffles, clean them well, peel them and cut them in small pieces; boil the skins for two minutes in a glass of sherry. Mince them together with two pounds of sausage meat, season well, add the pieces of truffle and stuff the bird. Roast in the ordinary way. Remove the fat before serving the gravy.

CANARD AUX OLIVES
Baked Duck

Roast the duck for about half an hour. Put in a saucepan a table-spoonful of *roux brun*, one of *consommé*, one of white wine; wash, peel, and stone a good many olives; add them to the sauce and cook a few minutes. This sauce being ready, finish cooking the duck in it.

CONFIT D'OIE
Preserved Goose

Take a piece of *confit d'oie*,[1] of the required size and brown it in its own fat in the frying pan. The *confit* being kept in fat, there is usually enough fat attached to each piece for the frying. Fry also with it some parsley till very crisp.

The *confits d'oie* can be served in the following manner:
1. With potatoes fried in the goose fat.
2. With a tomato sauce.
3. On a *purée* of sorrel.
4. With a *sauce piquante*.
5. With peas.

[1] See, for the preparation of *confit d'oie*, page 67. If you have no room for stock of that kind, you can buy it in tins. Each contains a leg or a wing, enough for about five or six people.

CASSOULET

Soak a pound of haricot beans for ten hours. Cook them on a slow fire with salt, pepper, and one onion for about two hours. Take half a pound of pork, half a pound of *confit d'oie,* and cut them in several pieces. Brown them in butter with salt, pepper and four heads of garlic chopped with parsley, a glass of white wine; add two tablespoonfuls of *purée* of tomatoes and cook one hour. Put in the beans, a few thin pieces of bacon, one pork sausage fried and cut in slices, and let it simmer another hour and a half. Put all this in a fireproof dish, sprinkle with breadcrumbs, add a few small pieces of butter and brown in the oven. Serve boiling hot in same dish.

PERDRIX AUX CHOUX
Braised Partridge

Get a nice white cabbage, cut it in four, remove the outside leaves and cook it for ten minutes in salted water. Remove it and drain it well.

Take a partridge (it need not be a young one), cut it in four pieces and put them in a saucepan with a good piece of butter, a carrot, one onion, a few small pieces of bacon, a pinch of flour, a spoonful of *consommé,* parsley, and cook for twenty minutes. Add the cabbage, a pork sausage cut in slices, and let it simmer till the flesh is quite tender. Then remove the partridge, the cabbage, bacon and sausage, and keep warm; let the rest reduce to a thick gravy, which you add, after having passed it through a sieve, to the dish.

LIÈVRE À LA ROYALE

Bone the hare. Prepare a stuffing with a pound of truffled *foie gras* cut in slices, a quarter of a pound of veal and pork mixed, salt and pepper; arrange the minced meat between the slices of *foie gras* and remodel the hare. Tie it well.

Put in a saucepan a good piece of butter, a few small onions and a handful of cut bacon (in little cubes). Cook for a few minutes, then brown your hare in this. Remove it; add a spoonful of flour and stir well, then three-quarters of a bottle of good claret, the blood of the hare (in which you have put a little claret or a few drops of vinegar to prevent its coagulating), parsley, salt and pepper.

Put the hare in à large pot made of thick iron (failing that, a thick fireproof dish), pour over it the mixture, and later add half a dozen truffles cut in slices. Cook on a very slow and even fire for twelve hours. Remove the string and parsley before serving.

This dish, a very ancient one, is one of the very best the South of France has produced. Needless to say, it is only made for great occasions. One can still see in certain kitchens the large pot made of thick iron used for the purpose. This is called a *milloquière* and I doubt if one could buy one now-a-days.

PICKLED MEATS AND PÂTÉS

PETIT SALÉ

Petit salé is a kind of pickled pork. It is usually made in large quantities at the time, as it keeps for a long time. But it can also be prepared in small quantities.

Take several pounds of pork, preferably from the neck or the breast, or the parts of the animal which are streaky. Cut them in pieces, about three or four inches long.

Get à large earthenware jar with an opening narrower than the bottom. Put at the bottom à layer of thyme and bay leaves, then a thick coat of salt. It is necessary to use the coarse grey salt, unrefined, sea salt being preferable to rock salt. Take a piece of pork and rub it well over with salt, then another, till you have made à layer of meat, all the pieces being well pressed against one another; then another thick layer of salt, and so on, till you have filled the jar or come to the end of your stock of pork. Cover the jar with a piece of cloth, then with the lid. If the jar has no lid, a piece of board over the cloth with something heavy over it will do. Keep in a cool place at least ten days before using.

When you take a piece, take it with your fingers; do not dig in the jar with a fork, and replace the salt carefully.

. . .

The other way of making *petit salé,* by pickling in *saumure,* is equally good. Take a jar, put bay leaves and thyme as before and fill it with water, leaving of course room for the pieces of pork. Put in salt, a handful at the time, and stir with a wooden spoon to make it dissolve. Go on adding salt till you reach the saturation point, that is to say, when the water cannot dissolve any more salt (which you will know by putting an egg in it; it floats if the water is saturated). Then put the meat in and keep covered in a cool place.

If you make à large quantity, do not forget when you reach the bottom pieces to wash them in several waters before using, otherwise, no doubt, they would be too salt.

CONFITS D'OIE
Preserved Goose

Take a well-fattened goose. Cut it in pieces, legs, wings, neck, breast, etc. Remove carefully all the fat attached, also the fat inside the bird. Put the meat for twenty-four hours in a jar with coarse salt, thyme and bay leaves. Melt the fat in à large saucepan with a spoonful of water and one pound of pork fat. When well melted, put in the parts of the goose and cook on very slow fire for four hours (drying the pieces well before you put them to cook). Then put them in an earthenware jar and pour the fat over. When cold, cover the jar as for *petit salé*. Your *confit* in a few days is ready for use.

When you want a piece take it out and see that none of the others are exposed to the air. It is advisable to melt again part of the fat and pour it afresh over the *confits*. They will keep for months. In Périgord the stock for the year is usually prepared about Christmas time.

Confits are also made with ducks and turkeys, and, after all, *petit salé* is only a cheaper and coarser form of *confits*.

RILLONS
Potted Pork

In the origin *rillons* were the scraps of meat left at the bottom of the big pan in which the meat of a whole pig was cooked for the purpose of making fat for the needs of the household. They were then seasoned and kept in small pots. But those days are over, and *rillons* are now made on a smaller scale.

Take several pounds of streaky pork, cut it in small pieces and roll them well in salt and lots of pepper. Put all this in à large saucepan with a tumblerful of salted water and cook on a moderate fire. Stir often to help the melting of the fat and the evaporation of the water. Cook till the pork meat is a nice brown colour. When the fat stops smoking it is cooked.

Remove them from the fire and squeeze through a sieve. Taste them, add more seasoning if necessary, put them back in the saucepan and cook a few minutes more. Then put them in earthenware pots and pour slowly the melted fat over them, so that it fills the tiny spaces left in the *rillons*. Go on pouring till you have on the top à layer of pure fat about half an inch thick. Cover with paper and the lid. *Rillons* are very good cold as a kind of coarse *pâté*, as *hors d'œuvre*, and also used for different dishes.

RILLETTES
Potted Pork

Variation on the same theme. Get several pounds of pork, some fat, some lean, chops or legs, and chop it very finely. Begin the cooking. Also boil in a *court-bouillon* without vinegar a piece of pig's liver (half a pound for about three or four pounds of *rillettes*); when well cooked pound it well, add it to the pork meat, mix well, add salt and a good deal of pepper. Bring to the boil, stirring all the time, and then cook more slowly till ready. Remove from the fire, stirring occasionally, so that the fat and the lean remain well mixed. Wait till the fat is half set to put in pots.

For both these *pâtés* the proportion of fat and lean is rather a question of taste. On the whole, the best is half and half, which you usually get in using the streaky parts of the pork for the *rillons,* and a pound of lean to a pound of fat for the *rillettes.*

PÂTÉ DE FOIE GRAS

Take half a pound of streaky pork, pass it through the mincing machine, add salt and pepper. Get three or four truffles, peel them and cut them in three or four pieces, chop the skins and add them to the minced meat. Take a *foie gras* (duck's or goose's) about one pound and a half in weight. Put in some truffles here and there.

Take a *terrine* or earthenware jar, coat the bottom of it with the minced meat; a few truffles, the *foie gras,* a few truffles, a coat of minced meat.

Cover the pot, cook about one hour and a quarter in a *bain marie* in a moderate oven. Let it get tepid, then press it slightly, drain whatever gravy there is in the jar and fill with melted pork fat or, better still, goose fat. A coat of pork fat on the top, a sheet of tin paper overlapping the edge, and put the lid on. Keep in a cool place, but not damp.

PÂTÉ DE VOLAILLE
Pâté of Chicken or Duck

Bone a chicken, and put aside the white meat. Mince the rest with half a pound of lean veal, half a pound of lean pork and a quarter of a pound of pork fat. Season well and add a few chopped truffles. Take a jar, put first à layer of minced meat, then alternately a very thin rasher of bacon, white meat of chicken, bacon, minced meat, and so on till the pot is full. Cook for one hour and a quarter in a *bain marie* in a moderate oven.

The same can be done with duck, in which case it would be a pity not to add some fine truffles, the peelings of which should be added, cooked for a few minutes in a liqueur glass of port wine to the minced meat. It should cook about a quarter of an hour longer.

Vegetables

POMMES DE TERRE FRITES
Fried Potatoes

Like all simple things, fried potatoes are often very badly done. They should be golden brown, crisp and dry, and served the moment they are ready. Never fry potatoes in a frying pan. You want a deep vessel full of fat (which must not be used for anything else). It is very important, after you have cut your potatoes in whatever shape you like best, to dry them well in a cloth. It is equally important that the fat should be very hot. Throw in your potatoes. They must be literally and freely swimming in boiling fat. When golden brown, remove them, drain them well and sprinkle with salt.

They are easily drained if you fry them in a wire basket. It is advisable to throw them on à large piece of white paper, which will absorb what is left of the fat. The sprinkling of salt will finish the drying besides giving them taste.

POMMES DE TERRE EN ROBE DE CHAMBRE

Take some large potatoes of the white floury kind, wash them well and cook in the oven. The skin must be crisp. Serve them with fresh butter or *rillons*.

POMMES DE TERRE FRITES AUX FONDS D'ARTICHAUX

Take three artichokes,[1] break off the leaves and the heart and only keep the bottom part, trim it well and cut it into four pieces. Add them to about three-quarters of a pound of potatoes prepared for frying. Fry together and sprinkle with salt.

POMMES DE TERRE SOUFFLÉES

Take some potatoes (the long Dutch kind) and cut them in thin slices (they should not be thicker than two half-a-crown pieces together); wipe them well. Drop them in the hot fat, not too many at the time; they must not stick together. Cook them three-quarters of the full time they ought to cook (by that time usually they come up and float on the top); then take them out. Leave the fat on the fire for two minutes more (it must reach that point when it begins to smoke); put them in again for a minute or two in a wire basket, and they will puff up at once. Make them a good colour, drain well, sprinkle with salt and serve quickly.

PURÉE DE POMMES DE TERRE

Wash, cut and put your potatoes (the white floury kind is the best) in salted water, bring to the boil. When cooked, drain the water well. Mash them, add salt and pepper, a piece of butter and a little boiling milk. Whip it well over the fire. The *purée* must be neither too thick nor too clear, and very light.

---

[1] I mean, of course, the real artichoke, not the vegetable mysteriously named Jerusalem artichoke.

GÂTEAU DE POMMES DE TERRE AUX OIGNONS

Cut two large onions in thin slices and fry them in butter till very brown. Add them to about a pound of potato *purée,* add a little more salt and pepper, and put the mixture, well worked, in a buttered fireproof dish. The dish should be rather flat and the mixture not more than three-quarters of an inch thick. Add a few pieces of butter on the top and brown well in the oven.

You can also do this dish in a frying pan, frying first one side, then the other. It gives it a slightly different taste.

POMMES DE TERRE MAÎTRE D'HÔTEL

Cook (in their skins) some potatoes in salted water, preferably the long yellow kind. Dry them well, peel them, cut them in slices. Melt in a flat saucepan a good piece of butter, add a drop of water, a little salt; add the potatoes, cook five minutes, add chopped parsley and serve.

POMMES DE TERRE BOULANGÈRE

Cut two large onions in thin slices, cook them for a few minutes only in butter. Cut your potatoes in thin slices, arrange them in a very flat dish with the onions, add a claret glass full of *consommé,* a good deal of pepper and salt, and brown in a moderate oven for about one hour and a half.

POMMES DE TERRE AU FROMAGE

Cook some potatoes in salted water, peel them and cut in slices. Prepare a *roux blanc,* to which you add grated cheese. Add the potatoes and mix well. Brown in the oven.

POMMES DE TERRE LYONNAISE

Cook the potatoes in salted water, peel them and cut them in slices. Keep them till they are just warm. Fry them in butter, add salt and pepper. Later add two onions finely sliced, so that potatoes and onions are ready and brown together.

POMMES DE TERRE SAUTÉES

Parboil the potatoes in salt water; peel them; wait till they are just warm and fry them in butter till nicely brown. Add seasoning and chopped parsley just before serving.

POMMES DE TERRE FARCIES

Peel and clean some large potatoes; make a hole in the centre and fill with stuffing made either of sausage meat or of remnants of cold meats, to which you add chopped garlic, a little bacon, parsley, salt and pepper. Put them in a fireproof dish with a piece of butter and a little *consommé*. Cook in a moderate oven, basting often.

CROQUETTES DE POMMES DE TERRE

Bake in the oven some large white potatoes. When cooked peel them and pass them through a sieve; add salt and pepper, a little butter and the yolks of two eggs. Work it well over the fire so as to dry it. Let it get half cold. Then make small *croquettes,* about one inch thick and three inches long, roll them in flour, and either bake in the oven or fry in butter.

POMMES DE TERRE NOUVELLES

Wash and scrape some new potatoes; dry them well. Melt some butter in a pan till golden only, put in the potatoes and cook them till lightly brown; put them in a fireproof dish with the butter and finish cooking in the oven. Serve with the butter in which they have cooked. Salt iust before serving.

POMMES DE TERRE NOUVELLES MAÎTRE D'HÔTEL

Boil your new potatoes in their skins. Drain well. Peel them and cover with a *maître d hôtel* sauce.

CHOUX FARCI
Stuffed Cabbage

Take à large white cabbage, boil it about a quarter of an hour in salted water. It must be cooked enough for you to open the leaves without breaking them. Remove it, drain it well and open it. Once open, stuff it with either sausage meat or the following mixture: sausage meat, veal, bacon, garlic, parsley shallots, minced together and highly seasoned. Give the cabbage its original shape and tie it with string. Put the prepared cabbage in a fireproof dish with butter, a spoonful of *consommé*, salt and pepper, and cook in a moderate oven, basting often. Remove the string before serving.

You can, if you like, make instead of one cabbage several miniature ones, by surrounding a ball of minced meat with a few leaves. It is rather better and easier to serve.

CHOUX DE BRUXELLES AU BEURRE
Brussels Sprouts

Put the Brussels sprouts in salted boiling water. Drain well. Put in a saucepan a good piece of butter, a drop of water, bring to the boil, put in the sprouts, add salt and pepper; cook five minutes and serve.

CHOUX DE BRUXELLES AUX MARRONS
Brussels Sprouts and Chestnuts

Prepare and cook as before, but add a quarter of the quantities of chestnuts, which have been parboiled first, then passed in butter.

CHICORÉE AU JUS
Chicory

Clean the chicory well, wash it in cold water, poach it for five minutes in boiling water. Drain it well by squeezing in a sieve, chop it, put it in a saucepan with salt, pepper, butter, a little *consommé, jus,* or gravy, and let it simmer for a little while.

ÉPINARDS AU JUS
Spinach

Prepare in exactly the same way, but cook a little longer. You can, if you like, add a tablespoonful of cream.

LAITUES AU JUS
Lettuce

Wash and clean your lettuces, keep only the heart, poach them five minutes in hot water. Drain them well. Put them in a dish with butter, a little *jus* or *consommé,* salt and pepper, and cook about a quarter of an hour in a covered dish or in a moderate oven, basting often.

ENDIVES AU JUS
Endives

Prepare and cook in exactly the same way, but a little longer.[1]

PURÉE D'OSEILLE
Sorrel

Wash and clean the sorrel, remove the hard portion of the bigger leaves, poach it in boiling water for about ten minutes. Drain it well, chop it, put it in a saucepan with a piece of butter, salt, pepper, and a tablespoonful of *consommé;* let it simmer for a little while.

---

[1] I find that English greengrocers call "endives" chicory and *vice versa*. The endive is the white unopened vegetable belonging to the dandelion species. The chicory is the curly salad with a slightly bitter taste. Gardeners tie it so that the inside leaves grow perfectly white.

ARTICHAUX À L'ITALIENNE
Artichokes

Take some artichokes, remove the leaves and the heart and keep only the bottom, which you trim well. Throw them in cold salted water. Boil them well and keep them in a cloth. At the same time prepare the following sauce: a tumblerful of *consommé,* a piece of butter the size of a walnut and a pinch of flour; mix well; cook slowly, then add a tablespoonful of grated cheese and a spoonful of white wine. Do this over the fire, stirring all the time. Cook about a quarter of an hour. Arrange the artichokes in a buttered dish, pour the sauce over, sprinkle with breadcrumbs and brown in the oven.

TOMATES FARCIES
Stuffed Tomatoes

Cut the tomatoes in two by the middle, remove the seed and salt them. Fill them with either of the following stuffings:

1. Chop an onion, brown it in butter, add chopped mushrooms, breadcrumbs, parsley, salt and pepper, a little *consommé.*
2. Chop an onion, brown it in butter, mix with sausage meat, add salt and pepper.

Fill the tomatoes, sprinkle with breadcrumbs, put a tiny piece of butter on each and cook in a moderate oven.

AUBERGINES FARCIES

Cut the *aubergines*[1] in two, scrape half the flesh, salt the inside and fry for a few minutes in very hot fat. Fill with a stuffing which is a mixture of the two described immediately above, with the addition of a little tomato sauce. Cook in the same way.

SALSIFIS SAUCE BLANCHE
Salsify

Scrape the salsify, wash them in water and a little vinegar. Put in a saucepan a handful of flour, add water little by little, mixing all the time. When you have enough liquid to boil your salsifis, salt and cook on a moderate fire till soft. Dry them and brown in butter, or serve with a *sauce blanche*. Salsifis are also very good in fritters, in which case you prepare them as before and dip them in batter before frying.

PETITS POIS
Peas

Take a pound of young small peas, put in a saucepan a tumblerful of water, a pinch of salt, the heart of a lettuce, two small onions and a piece of butter the size of a walnut. Bring to the boil, put in the peas and boil in an open saucepan on a quick fire. When cooked, remove the onions and lettuce and leave only a little juice; add half a tablespoonful of sugar, a little more butter, bring to the boil once and serve.

---

[1] *Aubergine* is that dark, purple vegetable, the correct English name of it being, I am told, "egg plant," anyhow, to be found at all decent greengrocers when in season.

HARICOTS FLAGEOLETS MAÎTRE D'HÔTEL

BUTTER BEANS

Cook the butter beans in salted boiling water with one onion. Pour out the juice, except for a tablespoonful, add a good piece of butter, salt, pepper, chopped parsley; bring to the boil and let it simmer twenty minutes and serve.

HARICOTS BLANCS

Haricot Beans

Take a pound of haricot beans. Soak them for twelve hours. Put them in a saucepan with lots of water, salt, broken pepper, one carrot, one onion, parsley; bring to the boil, skim well and let it simmer for three hours. Drain well, leaving only a tablespoonful of the juice, add butter and serve.

HARICOTS BLANCS EN PURÉE

Prepare and cook as before, but after draining pass through a sieve; then add butter and seasoning, working it over the fire. Should be the consistency of a potato *purée*.

The same can be done with any other dry vegetable, peas, lentils or broad beans.

CÊPES BORDELAISE

Wash and clean your mushrooms,[1] cut them in slices, and fry them in oil and butter, with salt and pepper, and shallots, garlic and parsley chopped together.

CÊPES PÉRIGOURDINE

Put the larger ones on the grill and grill them for a few minutes on both sides. With the smaller ones make a mince, adding chopped garlic and shallots, parsley, salt and pepper, and a drop of lemon juice. Put the Grilled mushrooms in an oiled dish, cover them with a thick coating of mince and brown in the oven.

CAROTTES À LA CRÈME

Take some small tender carrots, scrape and wash them. Put in a saucepan a small tablespoonful of flour, a good piece of butter, mix well, add a little milk, salt and pepper; mix well again, put in the carrots and cook slowly for about half an hour. Add a little cream just before serving.

CAROTTES SAUTÉES

Put in a dish a piece of butter[1] and fry the carrots; salt just before serving.

---

[1] Not usually gathered in England, but are to be found in tins at any grocer's in Soho and at most big stores.

CÉLERI AU JUS

Clean your celery, wash it well and remove the outside leaves. Poach it for about twenty minutes. Drain it well and cook like endives *au jus*.

CÉLERI AU FROMAGE

When boiled, put the celery into a fireproof dish with a covering of *béchamel* sauce and grated cheese. Brown in the oven.

CÉLERI FRIT

Cut in pieces the celery-root or celeriac after having washed and scraped well. Simply fry in butter or fat.

HARICOTS VERTS
French Beans

Get some French beans, break the ends and boil them in boiling water with salt and pepper. Drain them well, put them in a saucepan with a good piece of butter, salt and pepper, and cook them for a few minutes on a slow fire, shaking them often.

You can also serve them with a *maître d'hôtel* sauce, or fry them slightly in butter. They should be in any case rather highly seasoned.

PURÉE DE MARRONS
Chestnuts

Peel your chestnuts and boil them in salted water. Drain them and pass them through a sieve. Add a good piece of butter and a table-spoonful of *consommé*. Bring to the boil, stirring all the time, and let it simmer for a quarter of an hour. It should be rather thick.

MARRONS BLANCHIS
Steamed Chestnuts

Remove the thick skin only of the chestnuts and boil them ten minutes in salted water. Peel them and let them get nearly cold. Take a narrow and deep saucepan, put at the bottom water and a few potatoes and steam your chestnuts. Serve with fresh butter.

RIZ AUX PIMENTS
Rice and Peppers

Boil your rice and drain it well. It should be very dry and each grain separate. Take two or three *piments* or red peppers,[1] wash them, remove the seed, cut them in small pieces, add them to the rice with pepper and salt, a piece of butter, half a tablespoonful of *consommé,* and cook on a slow fire for a few minutes. You can, if you like the taste of it, add also a pinch of red saffron.

NOUILLES AU FOIE GRAS
Spaghetti

Boil some spaghetti[2] and drain it well. Take a buttered dish, put à layer of spaghetti, a little *purée* of *foie gras,* more spaghetti, more *foie gras,* finish with a good deal of grated cheese and a few pieces of butter. Brown well in the oven. It is not necessary for this dish to use the pure *foie gras;* the *purée,* which is sold in small tins, will do as well, provided it is the real thing and not pig's or calf's liver masquerading as *foie gras.*

---

[1] Piments, pimentos or red peppers, in season in the autumn, to be bought in tins almost anywhere.

[2] I know quite well that neither spaghetti nor *foie gras* are vegetables, but under which heading was I to put this altogether admirable dish?

OIGNONS À LA CRÈME

Boil in salted water three or four big onions. Dry them. Put in a fireproof dish one ounce of butter and melt it. Cut your onions in small quarters and put them in the butter till they get a golden colour; then add two rashers of streaky bacon cut very thin. Cook in the oven for a quarter of an hour. Remove the dish and keep it aside till it is only tepid. Then add one beaten egg, a spoonful of cream, mix well together and put back in the oven till golden brown.

PURÉE D'OIGNONS
Onions

Cook the onions in water and milk mixed in equal parts; add salt and a little nutmeg; when well cooked, drain them well and pass them through a sieve. Put the *purée* thus obtained in a saucepan, add a little butter, a *béchamel* sauce, and boil two minutes, stirring well.

TRUFFES AU XÈRÉS
Truffles in Sherry

Wash your truffles well in water, and brush them with a very hard brush to remove the earth which usually sticks to them. Peel them. Put them in a small saucepan with a pinch of salt and enough sherry to cover them well. The saucepan should be kept closed all the time they are cooking, that is, two hours on a very slow fire.

Truffles cooked in that way—or indeed in any way—should be eaten by themselves as a delicacy.

Needless to say, I am speaking of fresh truffles, which are in season only for a short time in the winter. Preserved ones are good enough for flavouring *pâtés* and *sauces,* but not for this special dish or the following one.

TRUFFES AU LARD
Truffles with Bacon

Wash and peel as before, salt them slightly and wrap each one in a very thin piece of streaky bacon. Wrap each again in three oiled papers well closed. Put them for three-quarters of an hour in a dish in a moderate oven. If you are lucky enough to have wood fires in your house, put the truffles under a heap of warm ashes, put a few burning cinders over them and cook for half an hour. That is the true and infinitely better way.

Salads

ONE cannot help wondering if an English salad is the result of ignorance or the aim of a curiously perverted taste.

A salad must be fresh and crisp, its flavour sharp and appetising. The ingredients with which it is made all have these qualities; so has the seasoning. Indeed, to make it sickly amounts to a *tour de force* which must be very difficult to accomplish.[1] Still, most English cooks seem to be very successful in their attempt with the help of cream sauces, sham *mayonnaises* and the addition of the fatal radish, the strong taste of which absolutely kills that of the other vegetables.

Rumour has it that, somewhere in America, they can make salads, though of a complicated kind and queer flavour; and I am assured by travellers that they taste more like strong cocktails than refreshing vegetable dishes.

I must give France its due. The French, I am told, have many failings, but they can make wine, coffee and salads. It is a great deal. French salads are of two kinds: the green salads, made with whatever is in season, simply dressed with oil, vinegar, pepper and salt; and the others, which are made more elaborately of fish, meat or vegetable, and which require a more elaborate dressing.

There is no doubt that, especially for a green salad, there is nothing better than oil made of crushed walnuts. It gives it a

---

[1] "I wish to God, ma'am, it were impossible!" as Dr. Johnson said about something else.

subtle flavour. Unfortunately, walnut oil is not now made in the farms and country houses as it used to be. There are very few places where you can buy it, even in France, so that the supply is very limited. The next best and more generally used is pure olive oil. No other oil except these two is any good. And, as I have remarked before, malt vinegar is worse than useless; if you have no wine vinegar you had better use the juice of a lemon. Of the wine vinegars, the one made of red wine is the best. This was well known, even in the sixteenth century; Rousard mentions it somewhere in a poem about salads:

L'arrouserons de vinaigre rosart.

THE DRESSING OF A SALAD

The best way is to melt the salt and the mustard (if mustard is used) in the vinegar in the spoon (ivory, bone or wood). Then sprinkle the pepper, then the oil. Stir lightly. The proportions are one and a half tablespoonfuls of vinegar to two and a half of oil. Green salads should be eaten the minute they are dressed; you would spoil the best salad by dressing it, say, just before dinner, and even a quarter of an hour makes all the difference in the freshness of the salad and the crispness of the leaves. A vegetable salad should be dressed one hour before serving, so that the dressing has time to penetrate the vegetables.

SALADE DE LAITUE
Lettuce

Plain dressing, no mustard, add chopped chervil and spring onions. Only the heart of the salad to be used.

SALADE DE CHICORÉE
Chicory

Plain dressing, rub the salad bowl with a piece of garlic, or put in it a small piece of toast rubbed with garlic.

SALADES D'ENDIVES

Plain dressing, cut the leaves in pieces, about two inches long.

SALADE DE CRESSON
Watercress

Plain dressing, only half a spoonful of oil, a few drops of lemon juice besides vinegar.

SALADE DE PISSENLIT
Dandelion

Plain dressing, only the whitest leaves of the dandelion.

SALADE DE SCAROLLE

Same as chicory.[1]

SALADE DE MÂCHES ET BETTERAVE
Corn Salad and Beetroot

Plain dressing. *Mâche* is called by green- grocers "corn salad," and by some dictionaries "lamb's lettuce."

[1] Is another kind of chicory, with larger and not curly leaves.

SALADE DE TOMATES
Tomato

Cut the tomatoes in thin slices. Season with plain dressing and chopped parsley.

SALADE DE CONCOMBRES
Cucumber

Peel the cucumbers, cut them in small slices, put them on a plate and sprinkle with salt. This will bring the water out of the cucumber. One hour afterwards drain them well and add pepper and vinegar, no oil.

SALADE DE BETTERAVES
Beetroot

Only salt, pepper and vinegar.

SALADE DE HARICOTS VERTS
French Beans

Break both ends of the French beans and cook in boiling water with salt. Drain them and put them in cold water. Dress with oil, vinegar, salt, pepper, one shallot and chervil chopped.

SALADE DE CHOUX-FLEUR
Cauliflower

When cold, remove all the hard parts of the cauliflower, break the rest in pieces. Dress with oil, vinegar, mustard, pepper and salt, one shallot and parsley chopped.

SALADE DE POMMES DE TERRE
Potato

When your potatoes are cold (the best kind for this is the long yellow kind), cut them in thin slices. Dress with oil and vinegar, pepper and salt, mustard, onion and parsley chopped (or shallots and chervil).

SALADE DE POMMES DE TERRE AUX PIMENTS
Potatoes and Peppers

Prepare as before, and add one-third of sliced *pimentos* or sweet red peppers. Add a few chopped gherkins.

SALADE DE POMMES DE TERRE AUX ANCHOIS
Potatoes with Anchovies

Prepare like an ordinary potato salad, and add half a dozen fillets of anchovies cut in small pieces.

SALADE DE BŒUF
Beef

Cut your boiled beef in thin pieces and then mix well with a *vinaigrette* sauce.

SALADE DE BŒUF AUX POMMES DE TERRE
Beef and Potatoes

Put pieces of beef and potatoes in equal quantities, dress with oil, vinegar, mustard, salt, pepper, chopped shallot and parsley.

SALADE DE BŒUF AUX HARENGS
Beef and Herrings

Small pieces of beef and cut fillets of herrings in equal parts. Dress with salt, pepper, very little oil, and instead of vinegar, the juice from the herrings. The kind of preserved herrings to be used for this is the kind called "Bismarck herrings" or *harengs marines,*[1] not the smoked fillets of herring in oil.

SALADE DE THON
Tunny Fish

Get a tin of *thon à l'huile* (tunny fish), break the fish in pieces and dress with vinegar and salt.

SALADE DE POISSON
Fish

Take remnants of any boiled white fish, dress with oil, vinegar, pepper, salt, a chopped shallot and parsley; a few leaves of lettuce round the dish.

SALADE DE CÉLERI
Celeriac

Cut in very thin slices some celeriac, dress with salt, pepper, oil, vinegar, and a good deal of mustard.

---

[1] To be found in tins or glass jars anywhere.

SALADE RUSSE

Boil carrots, potatoes, French beans, peas (they should be boiled separately, as they are not all boiled in the same way). When cold, cut them in very small cubes. Add also (cut in small cubes) ham, beetroot, cucumber. Season with salt and pepper, oil and vinegar. About one hour later add a *mayonnaise* sauce and mix well together.

SALADE D'ORGE ET D'ORANGES
Oranges and Barley

Boil some barley; peel some oranges, remove the skin of each quarter, dress with salt, vinegar, and very little oil.

SALADE DE CÉLÉRI ET DE POMMES
Celery and Apples

Two-thirds of celery to a third of apples. Cut very thin, ordinary plain dressing.

SALADE DE CÉLÉRI ET TRUFFES
Celeriac and Truffles

Cut the celeriac in very thin pieces; peel and cut the truffles in the same way. Dress with oil, vinegar, pepper and salt. There should be at least one-third of truffles to two-thirds of celeriac.

SALADE DE LÉGUMES. I
Mixed Vegetable Salad

Use same vegetables as for *salade russe,* but without ham or *mayonnaise* sauce.

SALADE DE LÉGUMES. II

Cut some tomatoes in slices, remove the seed; add a quarter of the quantity of beetroot. Dress with salt and pepper, mustard, oil and vinegar, chopped shallots and a teaspoonftil of rum.

SALADE DE LÉGUMES. III

Use half tomatoes, half sweet red peppers. Cut in slices. Dress with oil, vinegar, pepper, salt, mustard and chopped parsley.

SALADE DE LÉGUMES. IV

Take some branch celery, sweet red peppers, and cauliflower in equal quantities. Add a few slices of beetroot, half a dozen chopped gherkins, spring onions. Season with oil and vinegar, mustard, salt, and a good deal of pepper.

Sweets and Pastry

COMPÔTE DE POMMES
Compôte of Apples

Peel and cut the apples and cook them on a slow fire, adding a tumblerful of water and sugar. When reduced to a pulp and no water left at all, add a piece of butter the size of a small egg and a teaspoonful of apricot jam. Whip the mixture well. Cook for a few minutes more, stirring all the time. Serve cold.

POMMES AU FOUR
Baked Apples

Take some large cooking apples, remove the core and fill the empty space with butter. Put them in a fireproof dish with a claret glass of water and sugar. Also sprinkle them well with sugar. Bake in a moderate oven.

POMMES À LA CRÈME
Fried Apples

Cut the apples in quarters and brown them in butter. When cooked, sprinkle them with sugar and pour rum over them; set it alight. Add a little apricot jam to the juice. Serve with whipped cream to which you have added a little rum.

PÂTÉ À FRIRE
Batter for Fritters

Put half a pound of flour in a dish. Make a hole in the middle, put a pinch of salt, two tablespoonfuls of olive oil, the yolks of four eggs; add warm water little by little, stirring all the time, till you get the proper consistency (like cream); put a cloth over it, let it rest two hours, and just before using add the whites of two eggs well whipped.

If you want to use it for fruit fritters, add a little sugar and a port glass full of rum.

PÂTÉ FEUILLETÉE
Batter for Pastry

Take a quarter of a pound of flour, a quarter of a pound of fresh butter, half a tumblerful of water, a liqueur glass of rum, and a pinch of salt.

Put the flour on the board, make a hole in the middle, put in salt, rum, and a piece of butter the size of a walnut. Add the water little by little. Work it well with your hand quickly. Make a ball of the batter, roll it in flour, make a few cuts with a knife, wrap it in a cloth, and let it rest a quarter of an hour.

After which you roll the batter with the rolling pin, put in the middle the rest of the butter and cover it with the batter.

Put it on the board and roll it lightly; fold it again and roll. Cover with a cloth and let it rest a quarter of an hour. Do this operation twice more with an interval of fifteen minutes. It is ready for use.

GUICHE
Cheese Tart

Make your *pâté feuilletée* as described above. Butter a flat mould and put in the batter. Cook it in a hot oven for about twenty minutes and remove it.

Mix and beat well the following mixture: grated cheese, preferably Gruyère, not quite a quarter of a pound, one beaten egg, a tumbler of cream; put this mixture in your tart and cook about a quarter of an hour, till the cream is set and golden. You can, if you like, add a few pieces of bacon chopped fine.

BEIGNETS DE FRUITS
Fruit Fritters

Cut your fruit (apples, peaches or pineapple) in slices. Soak them for a little while in rum or kirsch, dip them in the batter and fry in very hot fat. Sprinkle with sugar and serve very hot.

BEIGNETS SOUFFLÉS
Puffed Fritters

Put in a saucepan half a pint of water, a pinch of salt, a teaspoonful of sugar, three ounces of butter, and bring to the boil. When the butter is well melted add a quarter of a pound of flour, mix quickly on a slow fire till you get the proper consistency. Dry it a little and remove it from the fire for ten minutes, add one by one six eggs. Stir and let it rest.

Take with a spoon a little batter, about the size of a walnut, and drop it in very hot fat. Cook till nicely brown. They should puff to the size of an apple. Sprinkle with sugar and serve at once.

CRÊPES
Pancakes

Put in a basin half a pound of flour, make a hole in the middle, add a pinch of salt, a little sugar, three eggs, a glass of rum (or brandy, or Grand Marnier, or curaçao); mix well and add warm water little by little, working the paste well till it is very smooth and the consistency of cream.

Put in a frying pan a small piece of butter. When it is getting brown, put in quickly a tablespoonful of batter, move the frying pan so that it covers the whole bottom (it should be as thin as possible) and cook both sides on a quick fire. Sprinkle with sugar, roll it and serve hot.

CRÊPES FOURRÉES
Stuffed Pancakes

Prepare your pancake as before, but instead of rolling it at once put it flat in a dish, and pour over it a little vanilla cream or apricot jam, then roll it loosely, sprinkle with sugar and burn it with a red-hot iron.

SOUFFLÉ AUX MARRONS
Chestnut Soufflé

Prepare the chesnuts as for *marrons blanchis*, peel them and mash them through a sieve. Put the *purée* in a saucepan with a spoon-ful of cream, a little butter and sugar to taste, bring to the boil on a slow fire, and cook a few minutes. Remove it from the fire; add the yolks of five eggs and work it well; let it get tepid; whip the whites of five eggs, add them to the mixture and cook in a buttered soufflé-dish in a moderate oven for a quarter of an hour.

SOUFFLÉ

Prepare in the same way, using ground rice instead of chestnuts, and milk instead of cream. Can be flavoured with chocolate, orange, vanilla, or *maraschino*. Can also be done with grated cheese, *purée* of haddock, of sorrel or spinach.

OMELETTE AU RHUM

Prepare your eggs in the ordinary way and add castor sugar. Mix well, and use the mixture without delay; otherwise the omelette will be a failure. Put in the pan a little more butter than for an ordinary omelette. Fold it as usual, sprinkle with sugar and burn it with a red-hot iron. Warm some rum, pour it over the omelette and light it. It should burn for a few minutes or the flavour of rum will be too strong.

MILLAS GIRONDIN

This is a kind of custard, as done in the Bordeaux district. Chop four or five bitter almonds and boil them in a pint of milk. Take three spoonfuls of flour, the yolks of three eggs, two or three spoonfuls of sugar and add to this a little cold milk. Mix it well. Add to it the whites of three eggs, well whipped. Work it all well together and add the pint of hot milk. Put it in a mould and cook *au bain marie* in a fairly hot oven.

GALETTE AU CHOCOLAT
Chocolate Cake

Take a quarter of a pound of chocolate, melt it by the fire, mix with it the yolks of three eggs, about a quarter of a pound of sugar, two ounces of butter, then two spoonfuls of flour. When all this is well mixed, add the whites of the eggs well whipped. Butter one flat fireproof dish and put in the mixture; it should be about one inch thick. Cook ten minutes in a hot oven. When nicely golden, turn it over in another buttered dish and cook another ten minutes The inside of the cake should remain soft.

PAIN D'EPICES
Gingerbread

Put in a basin half a pound of flour, a quarter of a pound of crystallised sugar, a quarter of a pound of brown honey, a teaspoonful of bicarbonate of soda, a pinch of caraway seed powder, and a pinch of ginger powder. Add a teacupful of boiling water and mix well. To be cooked in a moderate oven for about one hour and a half in buttered tins with the lid on. Old cigarette boxes (50 or 100 size) would serve the purpose.

MOUSSE AU CHOCOLAT
Chocolate Mousse

Whip the cream lightly till it is stiff enough. Add a little sugar and melted chocolate (the consistency of syrup). Let it rest half an hour before serving. Can be flavoured with coffee, or orange instead of chocolate.

PRUNEAUX AU VIN
Stewed Prunes in Claret

Boil your prunes in water and sugar on a slow fire; put in half a vanilla pod. When the water is well reduced and the prunes about three-quarters cooked add a good glass of claret and simmer till the juice is the consistency of a syrup. Before serving remove the vanilla pod, wash it. and dry it well; it can be used several times.

FRAISES AU BORDEAUX
Strawberries

Clean the strawberries, remove the stalks, sprinkle with sugar, and add a tablespoonful of good claret or white wine. Cream should not be served with this.

SALADE DE FRUITS
Fruit Salad

Take a good-sized melon, preferably a cantaloup. Cut open the top, remove all seeds and scoop out the flesh with a silver spoon. Mix together strawberries, raspberries, apricots cut in small pieces, peaches, some of the melon flesh, a few green almonds, add sugar and a liqueur glass of kirsch. Put it all back in the melon and let it stand a quarter of an hour in a cool place. This salad should be made, of course, only with fresh fruit.

Sundries

CORNICHONS
Gherkins

Take some small gherkins, brush them well and clean them, cut off the stalks. Put them in a dish with a good deal of coarse salt and leave them twenty-four hours. Dry them well. After that they are ready to be put in glass jars with: two red peppers, bay leaf, two onions, parsley, tarragon, pepper and pure, strong wine vinegar. Cover the jars. They are ready about three weeks later, and, if the vinegar is good, will keep over a year.

SIROP DE CAFÉ
Syrup of Coffee

Make your coffee, using two ounces of coffee for a pint and a quarter of water. Dissolve in the coffee one pound of sugar and put in a little vanilla. Boil it for three minutes. Remove from the fire and add a spoonful of rum.

CAFÉ
Coffee

There is only one way of making good French coffee, and no amount of complicated utensils will improve on it. The right proportion of coffee is a heaped-up tablespoonful to a cup. Put it in the filter and pour over it the boiling water little by little. As the water goes through slowly, it is advisable to stand the coffee pot in boiling water. It is absolutely useless to make the water go through several times, as all the goodness and colour from the coffee is extracted by the very first water which goes through. It is dangerous to stand the coffee pot on a gas ring, as the coffee might boil and all the aroma would disappear. It takes quite a quarter of an hour to make enough coffee for four people, which, I suppose, explains why so many people do not take the trouble to do it well.

ESSENCE D'ORANGE ET DE CITRON
Essence of Orange and of Lemon

The rind of oranges peeled off very thin, to be put in a glass jar with alcohol at 90 or 95 degrees, enough to cover the skins, but no more. Leave it at least a month, shaking occasionally, then remove the pieces of rind. It makes a pure essence of orange, extremely scented and strong. A teaspoonful would be enough to flavour a sweet; and a few drops in a glass of water with a lump of sugar makes a very refreshing summer drink, at a time when oranges are at their worst. Lemon rind to be treated in the same way.

ORANGEADE

Squeeze the juice out of six oranges, add a tumblerful of water, sugar to taste, a claret glass mixed of kirsch and Grand Marnier (or kirsch and Benedictine); let it stand for an hour or so in a cool place. Add at the last minute soda water in sufficient quantities to make about eight tumblers full.

LEMONADE

The juice of five lemons, a little plain water, a claret glass full of gin (or whisky or brandy), sugar to taste. Let it stand one hour. Add soda water just before serving.

LAIT D'ANANAS
Pineapple Wine

The juice of a good-sized pineapple, a tumblerful of barley water (rather thick), a claret glass of kirsch, sugar to taste. Let it stand one hour in a cool place. Add soda water just before serving.

GELÉE DE COINGS
Quince Jelly

Peel and cut the quinces in quarters (put them in water as you do so, otherwise they will get black), dry them well. Put them in a saucepan with a little water and cook them on a moderate fire till reduced to a pulp. Pass through a sieve, and add the same weight of sugar as there is of quince juice. Boil about twenty minutes, skimming well. Put in pots in the ordinary way.

CONFITURES DE TOMATES
Tomato Jam

Choose some fine tomatoes, peel them, remove the seed and weigh the fruit. Take the same weight of sugar with enough water to dissolve it; boil it a few minutes, skimming well; put in the tomatoes, cook them about two hours, stirring occasionally; about half an hour before removing them put in a vanilla pod. When cooked, remove the vanilla and fill your pots, covering like any other jam. This tomato jam has a very delicate flavour.

CRÈME DE CAMEMBERT

Get a good, ripe Camembert and scrape it well. Put it in a dish and cover it with white wine; leave it for twelve hours. Scrape it again and dry it well. Mix with half the amount of butter, beating it till absolutely smooth. Give it its original shape and sprinkle with breadcrumbs.

It is preferable to use a real Camembert. Every shop will tell you that theirs is the real Camembert. As a matter of fact, the box containing the genuine Camembert bears printed in a square in the middle of the pattern the words: *Syndicat des fabricants de Camembert de Normandie.*

A Week's Menu

SUNDAY

LUNCHEON
Soft roes omelette
Grilled cutlets
French beans
Potatoes boulangère
Cheese and fruit

DINNER
Vegetable soup
Cold roast pork périgourdine
Fried potatoes
Salad of peppers and cauliflowers
Compote of apples

MONDAY

LUNCHEON
Hors d'oeuvre
Roast pork périgourdine
Potato purée
Cheese and fruit

DINNER
Pot-au-feu
Risotto with peppers
Roast chicken
Green salad
Endives au jus
Cheese tart

TUESDAY

LUNCHEON
Mackerel maître d'hôtel
Hachis parmentier
Cheese and fruit

DINNER
Sorrel soup
Fillets of sole
Chicken au gratin
Vegetable salad
Apple fritters

WEDNESDAY

LUNCHEON
Poached eggs béarnaise
Escalopes of veal
Peas à la française
Cheese and fruit

DINNER
Fish soup
Roast mutton
Soubise sauce
Sauté potatoes
Purée of spinach au jus
Chocolate mousse

THURSDAY

LUNCHEON
Boiled eggs
Tomato sauce
Brochette of liver
Lyonnaise potatoes
Cheese and fruit

DINNER
Julienne soup
Scallops
Roast beef
Stuffed tomatoes
Potato fritters
Orange soufflé

FRIDAY

LUNCHEON
Eggs en cocotte
Cold meat
Salade russe
Cheese and fruit

DINNER
Tomato cream
Mutton sauce piquante
Potatoes maître d'hôtel
Brussels sprouts and chestnuts
Macaroni au foie gras

SATURDAY

LUNCHEON
Turbot au gratin
Saute of beef
Chicory purée
Cheese and fruit

DINNER
St. Germain soup
Sole au vin blanc
Veal chop cream sauce
Soufflé potatoes
Salad of tomatoes and beetroot
Rum omelette

It will be noted that there are only three joints (pork, mutton, beef) and one chicken during the week. Now, if we look at the menus on the first day, we will see that:

The soup on Sunday evening is made with the bone out of the roast pork.

The roast pork is served again for Monday luncheon.

The *hors d'oeuvre* at that meal is made of the vegetable and bits of meat out of the soup, nicely arranged as a salad.

There was enough left in the tin of red peppers opened on Sunday evening for the salad to make the *risotto* for Monday dinner.

The *hachis parmentier* for Tuesday luncheon is made with the scraps of the roast pork and the boiled beef from Monday evening soup.

The main dish for Tuesday evening is made with what is left of the chicken arranged with potatoes *au gratin*.

The menus are completed by eggs, fish and small pieces of meat, according to requirements. We now reach Wednesday evening, when we have roast mutton, and Thursday, when we have roast beef. We will keep the best slices of both for a dish of mixed cold meat for Friday luncheon; the mutton will appear once more for Friday dinner, prepared with a *sauce piquante;* and the beef on Saturday for luncheon *sauté* with onions. So that the week, in spite of certain other dishes, the possible (or impossible) price of eggs, and the quantity of butter used to cook the dishes perfectly, will be considerably cheaper than if more meat had been used and the vegetables cooked only in water.

Menu for a Late Supper

AFTER AN INFORMAL PARTY

Soupe aux choux
Mixed cold meats
Salad
Dessert coffee

Nothing better, say at 3 o'clock in the morning, than a boiling hot *soupe au choux* and cold meat, with a very fresh, crisp salad. And you should drink with this one of those little white or pink wines from Anjou or Touraine, which have such a pleasant, sharp taste. Strong, black coffee on the top of it and you will feel ready to start again, whatever you may have been doing, or walk home all the way.

This is more suitable, though, for Chelsea than for Bayswater—unless the inhabitants of this "highly desirable district" happen to feel, for once, "delightfully Bohemian."

A Few Remarks About Wine

Je ne connais rien de sérieux, ici-bas, que la culture de la vigne.
—VOLTAIRE.

IT IS advisable to buy your wine from a reputable wine merchant; you are more likely to obtain the genuine article than at the next door grocer's. After all, there is no reason why an English grocer should know anything about wine.[1]

In any case, never buy wines labelled ever so vaguely Beaune, Pommard, St. Julien, St. Emilion; these names mean nothing, and the labels no doubt cover a multitude of doctored wines. If you do not know anything about it, and cannot afford château-bottled wines, let your wine merchant advise you about his cheaper vintages. It is in his interest as well as yours.

The only sound and cheap way is to buy wines about two years ahead of your requirements. Then you will get, for a moderate price, a wine which will improve both in quality and in value.

Your cellar should be dry, and of equable temperature, about 55 degrees Fahr. If you have no cellar, leave the bulk of your wine at your wine merchant's, who no doubt will store it for a nominal charge; and keep a few dozen bottles, in a cupboard for instance, not subject to vibration and strong daylight and far from any heating apparatus. The bottle should, of course, be kept on its side.

---

[1] They usually do not. I saw in quite an important shop *Beaujolais* (which is the name of a Rhône district) appear as a claret vintage. In another shop, the man to whom I was asking what wines they stocked, answered that they had "Burgundies and Gilbeys" (*sic*).

. . .

Red wines in England are nearly always served too warm. They should not be warmed at all, either by standing the bottle near the fire, or, worse still, in hot water. The heat kills the flavour of the wine and makes the alcohol it contains become overpowering. That little sentence, "have the chill taken off", has done more harm to good wine than it is possible to imagine.

The wine should be simply chambré—that is, at the temperature of the room, no more.

You bring up your wine about seven hours before the meal, being careful not to shake it, and stand it (to allow the deposit to settle) in the room. About one hour before serving, uncork it and decant it very carefully into a slightly warm decanter. It is very important that there be not a drop even of the same wine left in the decanter from the night before.

In decanting you must be careful not to stir the deposit; you can easily see how far you can decant by doing the operation over a light. Then leave the decanter in the room, on the mantelpiece if you like, but not nearer the fire than that. Take out the stopper for about a quarter of an hour, just before dinner.

White wines must be served at the temperature of the cellar, that is, brought up just before the meal. You can ice them slightly in the summer, but not by putting ice in your glass.

Use rather thin glasses, slightly narrower at the top than at the bottom (and fill them only to two-thirds); this shape is the best, as it exposes a larger surface of the wine to the air and encloses the aroma. Also, pray do not swallow hastily your wine, as if it were a nasty medicine, but bear in mind Dr. Middleton's remark: "I shall hurry my drinking of good wine for no man."

Index

Index